CHINESE TRIBUTE

FIAT LUX

THIS VOLUME WAS PRESENTED
TO THE
UNIVERSITY OF LETHBRIDGE
LIBRARY

In memory of
Roy Parry Gabbott

The Author at Peking, 1934

Chinese Tribute

by C. A. S. Williams
Commissioner of Customs, China (retired)

LITERARY SERVICES AND
PRODUCTION LTD

© C. A. S. Williams, 1969
First published in 1969 by
Literary Services and Production Ltd,
26 Old Brompton Road, London SW7

Printed in Great Britain by
W & J Mackay & Co Ltd, Chatham, Kent

85321 007 1

Contents

Illustrations

Foreword

I will not dwell extensively on my early recollections, but I should like to explain that I have been connected in a bond of sympathy with the East from the time of my birth in Bushire, at the top of the Persian Gulf, in 1884.

My father and my uncle were Superintendents in the Indian Government Telegraphs. The latter wrote a Manual of Telegraphy which was used as a Government textbook.

One of my ancestors was Mary Bird, who went to Persia in 1891 and is noted for the exploration and medical work she carried out in that country. We are also related to William Wilberforce, who was responsible for securing the freedom of the African negro. The tomb of John Bird Sumner, Archbishop of Canterbury, another relative, may be seen in the Cathedral. My aunt, Francis Maria Williams, was a missionary teacher in China and author of a book, *A New Thing*, published in 1895. Such is my background.

My childhood was spent in India and the first language I spoke really fluently was Hindustani. It was rather convenient to be able to speak to the natives. I remember going with my parents to a garden-party in India, given by Lord and Lady Dufferin, where I disappeared and was eventually run to earth in the servants' quarters, surrounded by an admiring group of khidmugars and punkahwallahs who were regaling me with innumerable ice-creams and fancy cakes at my imperative command. They were astounded at my capacity!

From my ayah and bearer I assimilated a good deal of Oriental imagery. Though I had no Eastern blood in my veins, I was vaccinated from a black baby who had smallpox. Perhaps, in this way, I was inoculated with the mystery and spirit of Asia! The baby died, but I survived.

When I was six and my brother four years old our mother took us to England on a sailing-ship which was also carrying a consignment of Indian snakes and monkeys for the zoo. The monkeys were most amusing, especially when poked with a stick, but one of the pythons escaped and my mother found it coiled round a hot pipe in the bathroom! This gave her as great a shock as when she found me one day in India sitting in the bath and playing with a deadly tarantula which I was happily sailing in a toy boat!

On arrival in England we were left at a school of the Squeers variety, in Weston-super-Mare and our mother returned to India.

It was a long time before I forgot my Hindustani, and I often used to talk to my brother in that language. Hence I became known to my schoolmates as 'that Eastern-tongued fellow'!

After a few years of tribulation our parents discovered that we were being harshly treated at our school and badly fed as well. Moreover, I think we had fully covered the rather inadequate curriculum provided. We were accordingly removed and sent to Taunton House School at Brighton, and later to St Marks, Windsor, afterwards known as the Imperial Services College, where I eventually became Captain, and was presented to the late Queen Victoria when she drove from Windsor Castle to pay a visit of inspection to the College, in which she took a great interest.

We had permission to visit the Castle, and I once went to the long chamber over the Henry VIII gateway, where my grandfather, Major Geraghty of the Lancashire Fusiliers, and Military Knight of Windsor Castle, who lived there, died playing the violin at a dance. The band played on the Castle terrace, which was bright with flowers and ornamental shrubs.

The great Queen died shortly before I finished my education and the College boys were provided with special seats on the green slopes within the Castle walls in order to witness the funeral procession. The coffin was borne on a gun-carriage drawn by six horses, which took fright at the crowds and began to plunge about on the cobble-stoned road in a most alarming manner. However, as quick as thought, a number of sailors, on guard along the route, unlimbered the horses and drew the gun-carriage themselves.

Another memory of my schooldays is that I had the pleasure of hearing Mr Winston Churchill deliver one of his early public speeches when he was a young man of about twenty-six. He delivered a lecture to us on the experiences of his life when a war correspondent, how he was taken prisoner by the Boers in November 1899 and escaped a month later. This was before he entered Parliament.

I had always wanted to return to the East, and finally the opportunity arrived. This is my tribute to an Oriental country which I have had the honour to assist in the levy of tribute from others for a period of thirty-two years.

During my work in China I could not help being struck by the fact that the foreign establishment of the Maritime Customs Service, was largely responsible for the gradual development of the country and many of its public utilities, both under the Imperial regime and since the inauguration of the Republic.

At the same time I realized that life and sport in the Celestial Kingdom provided unique facilities for study and enjoyment.

My reactions to these circumstances, and the observations I made, are hereby put on record in the hope that they will be of some interest and entertainment, not only to those who are directly concerned with China, but also to the reading public in general.

1 September 1969   C. A. S. WILLIAMS

CHAPTER 1

The Receipt of Custom

'What sort of work has to be done in the Chinese Customs?' That was the problem which preoccupied me in 1903, when, after six months' study in France, I came to the conclusion that foreign languages, and travel and adventure in other countries, were more to my taste than anything else. I was nineteen at the time, and when I received a nomination through Sir Claude Macdonald, British Minister for China, to enter an examination for the Chinese Imperial Maritime Customs Service, I jumped at the chance.

I was, nevertheless, anxious as to the nature of the work. 'Don't you know?' one of the other candidates remarked. 'Why, you just sail up and down on a steam-launch, smoking a fat cigar!'

Strange though it may seem, this facile description held a modicum of truth, but it took me twenty-five long years before I eventually realized such a comfortable ambition. By that time I was Deputy Commissioner at Kowloon, and it was part of my duty to go round inspecting the various Customs stations in that district. As for the cigar, it was certainly missing when the sea was rough, as often happened.

Having passed the entrance examination, I was provided with a steamer passage to China. On arrival at Hong Kong on the 17th November, 1903, I reported to the Commissioner of the Kowloon district. He informed me that there were no orders, and I was to proceed to Shanghai and report there.

When I reached China proper, I found that the imperial form of government was still being carried on in the archaic manner with all its pomp and ceremony. The life of the common people was chiefly very primitive, however, except where it came under foreign influence.

The Emperor Kwang Hsü was inclined to agree to the reform of the traditional ways of the Empire by reorganizing the country on foreign lines, but the Empress Dowager T'zu Hsi, heading the Conservative Party, had virtually confined him to the Forbidden City at Peking, and held the reins of control herself.

The Tsungli Yamen, or Foreign Office, contained a certain number of progressive officials, and had great confidence in the foreign establishment of the Imperial Maritime Customs Service, which came under its authority.

It was understood between the Yamen and the Service that, as long as British trade predominated, there should be a British Inspector-General of Customs.

At Shanghai I reported to Sir Robert Bredon, Deputy Inspector-General, and he kindly invited me to lunch at the Shanghai Club. He asked me to meet him in the bar-room.

The Club is situated on the Bund, or river bank, and is well equipped with library, billiards tables, etc. Its bar had the reputation of being the longest one in the world. In any case, many of the local Taipans, or merchants of the international settlement, spent a long time there every day, and much business was transacted between drinks, which were regarded as a profitable investment. A pleasant life, I thought—but apt to be somewhat hard on the liver!

After a suitable aperitif we took our seats in the dining-room. I at once seized the opportunity of asking Sir Robert for some information regarding the organizing and functions of the Customs Service. He handed me a cigar, 'So it must be true,' I thought. 'I wonder where we shall find the steam-launch!'

However, it seemed my Customs duties had not yet started. Sir Robert briefly sketched the origin and nature of the Service.

'The foreign trade of China,' he began, 'may be traced back to about A.D. 1200, and taxation was paid to the Chinese Government by foreign merchants, chiefly in Canton, but under various difficulties and restrictions.'

'Was it on account of these difficulties that the collection of duty was taken over by the British and others?'

'Yes and no,' he replied, 'but it was in 1854, owing to the dislocation of trade caused by the Taiping rebellion, and the virtual collapse of the Customs system, that the Consuls for Great Britain, America, and France took control as a Board of Inspectors of Customs affairs in co-operation with the local Chinese Superintendent at Shanghai. It was found to be necessary to obtain Custom House officials with the necessary qualifications, as to probity, vigilance and knowledge of foreign languages, required for the enforcement of a close observation of treaty and Custom House regulations.'

'Did the Chinese of those days not have sufficient knowledge of foreign languages?' I inquired.

'No, very few spoke anything but pidgin English, which was not easily understood except by those accustomed to it, so the only adequate remedy was the introduction of a foreign element into the Custom House establishment, in the persons of foreigners carefully selected for this purpose. The Board became reduced to one British Inspector-General and so it continued.'

The Service was not, I gathered, by any means confined to the collection of duty. It also undertook many other activities at the request of the Chinese Government. For instance, postal departments were opened at various Custom Houses in 1878 (it was not until 1911 that the Postal Service was formed as a separate entity).

Another branch of the Service was the Marine Department, which eventually was provided with some twenty-six preventive sea-going vessels and thirty-three preventive launches, manned by 1,200 officers and men, including 130 foreigners. The lighting and buoying of the coast was also undertaken by the Customs.

The total staff of the Revenue and Marine Departments consisted, in 1935, of about 10,000 men, of whom some 700-odd were subjects of various foreign nations.

The Customs revenue, under this specialized international administration, gradually rose from a very small sum to about three hundred and forty million dollars, or twenty million, four hundred thousand pounds sterling at the exchange ruling in 1936, and constituted one of the most important assets in the budget of the Chinese Republican Government.

Besides giving me information about the Service, Sir Robert told me what furniture I should require to take to my first station, Hankow. It seemed I should be quartered in the Bachelors' Mess, which was not provided with bedroom furniture, though common-room and dining-room were fully equipped.

He also gave me this piece of useful advice. He said, after wishing me luck and shaking me by the hand:

'Always try to please your Chief, and never do anything he doesn't like.'

A good deal of water has flowed down the Yangtze River since I travelled on it by paddle-steamer to Hankow in those early days. I reached that busy port in the middle of the autumn race meeting.

My Chief, a burly, black-bearded Commissioner of my own nationality, looked to me very much like Henry the Eighth, and was in a very good humour, thanks to his substantial winnings at the Racecourse. He was smoking a large cigar.

I told him at once that I had decided never to do anything he didn't like.

His merry laugh rang out long and loud. 'Well, my boy,' said he, 'as long as you don't make any mistakes in the office, you can swear, drink and gamble as much as you like when you get home!'

I told him I was practically a teetotaller. He was very much astonished, and remarked that in all his varied experience he had never heard of a teetotaller coming to Hankow before!

Another young Assistant came to Hankow while I was there, and went to report to the Commissioner in his office. The Commissioner was very busy writing a dispatch, so the newcomer sat down in a free and easy manner, put his feet up on the desk, and lit a very strong cheroot!

'Young fellow,' said the Commissioner, 'do you realize where you are?' Perhaps it was the cheroot that was out of order?

'Sure,' he replied airily, 'I'm right here!'

'Yes,' said the Commissioner, 'but not for long. You get *right out of here*, finish your poisonous weed, come back, and keep your feet down!'

Hankow means 'Mouth of the Han River', a tributary which discharges into the Yangtze at that point, some six hundred miles from the coast. Walking along the foreshore, I could see the town of Wuchang, a mile across on the other side.

My work at Hankow consisted in the passing of export applications, and I soon realized that it was necessary to acquire some knowledge of the articles of the China trade. The notes I made from the export work, I entered in a loose-leaf notebook with an alphabetical index. This notebook often came in useful for purposes of reference in later years.

Thus I was safely launched on my new career. Did I say safely? Anyway, figuratively and literally my boats were burnt, for I heard that the steamer *Mei An*, on which I had travelled to Hankow, was destroyed by fire on her return trip to Shanghai! This was not my fault, I hoped. Had I left the burning end of my cigar on some inflammable deck cargo? But no, I ascertained that a Chinese passenger inadvertently upset an opium lamp as he stirred in his blissful state of dreamy oblivion. He and some other dope fiends lost their lives and never knew it!

The *North China Daily News* gave an account of this disaster, and also, curiously enough, it reported that the old Palace Hotel, where I had just been staying at Shanghai, had been burnt to the ground as well. I did a lot of cigar-smoking there, too, but I am glad I left before the smoke began to spread!

As a proof that all misfortunes occur in sets of three, the Hankow Custom House caught fire, and I began to think I was rather a Jonah! However, I worked all night helping to save the office and its archives and we succeeded in averting any serious damage—except to myself, as I fell through the roof of a warehouse, commonly known as 'go-down' (from the Malay *Gedang*). To me I must confess it was rather a *come-down*! When I came to, and emerged from the ashes—like a Phoenix reborn—I was considerably bruised and black and blue, chiefly on account of the smoke and the leakage from a barrel of indigo. But I certainly started my service in the Customs in a blaze of glory!

Nevertheless I decided to stick to my cigar, as originally advised. I wondered if it would be safer when I got my steam-launch.

CHAPTER 2

A Sense of Duty

We were four in the Bachelor's Mess at Hankow; one Russian, one American, and two British. We were all very friendly, but I suppose I naturally gravitated towards my own compatriot. He was a Second Assistant, A, and therefore eight ranks higher than I, who was only Fourth Assistant, C.

'In the Customs Service,' he said to me one day, 'it's most important to cultivate a sense of duty.'

I wondered whether he was pulling my leg and making a subtle joke, but he seemed quite serious.

This led to a discussion on the Staff in general and the work carried on in different departments. The Indoor Staff was our particular branch, where the Assistants attended to the levy of duty on goods examined by members of the Outdoor Staff. The latter also boarded and searched the vessels plying to and from the port, and were often recruited from men who had been to sea. As a Service we had specialized knowledge of ships and their cargoes. Though we were certainly a mixed collection of many nationalities, we all pulled together in the interests of the revenue and did our best to maintain the prestige of the Service.

I sat at the receipt of custom in the Hankow office one hot summer day. It was nearly closing time. The old side-wheel steamers *Kiangfoo*, *Hwalee*, and many others, with the all-seeing eye painted on the bows, were all cleared, and through the window came the raucous chanting of the transport coolies, 'Ai ya-ah lo-ah, lo-o-ah-ha oh-ha!' followed by a short pause to gather breath for a long-drawn 'AI-YEE', as they carried the miscellaneous cargo, slung from bamboo poles, to the pontoons on the foreshore. Strange scents drifted in from the surrounding native city—boiling oil, raw hides, lacquer, dried ducks, joss-sticks and, open drains. Each town in China, I was to find, has its own special aroma, chiefly governed by the local industrial activities, so many of which are conducted in the open air. Not quite time to pack up yet. I opened the drawer of my desk to put away my blue pencil and ships' manifests. It was very untidy, and evidently had not been cleared out for some considerable time. 'T'ing-ch'ai' (Office-boy), I called, 'sao kan ching' (clean this up). He did so, and in the process clouds of dust arose through which I watched a curious collection of antique rubbish emerging from hidden depths, some of it evidently dating back as far as the early Ming Dynasty. In later years I was often to have Augean stables to clean. Amongst the strange medley I found a piece of paper, yellow with age, inscribed with the following verses describing the composition of the Chinese Customs Service International Staff, their *camaraderie* and general sense of duty.

This seemed to be worthy of study, so I rescued it from oblivion, and record it herewith. I should like to have met the author, to whom I am greatly indebted.

A LEGION IN FAR CATHAY

Dedicated with great respect, and all good fellowship, to the Members of that most unique Service, the Imperial Maritime Customs of China; whose intelligence may be gathered from the good books in their libraries and the good whisky at their bars.

I

We're eleven hundred strong in numbers—a legion in far Cathay—
Collecting the Maritime Customs and in an Emperor's pay,
Who has never seen us nor wants to, so long as we gather the taels
Levied on Indian opium, on cotton and piece-goods bales.
With a Briton for a chieftain—a square man down to the ground,
Who can fine, suspend, and dismiss us, and shift and shuffle us
        round—
We are Russians, Britons and Frenchmen, and all the nations
        between,
But as loyal to our Master as Tommy Atkins to his king.

II

We're about as hot as they make 'em, a medley rich as is found,
Who've served under all the colours hoisted the whole world round.

We've romped across all the oceans and bruised the heads of the
   sea,
By the bluff old bows of a ditcher or a clipper caught by the lee;
Have served in most of the navies and fought in the 'thin red line',
We've faced the steel of the Sepoys, and dug in a silver mine,
Been 'sallying the ship' in an ice-field, harpooning whales by night,
Can do our bit in a skirmish, pitched battle, or free fight.

III

We've fought in foreign legions all along the Pacific coasts,
Been engaged a dozen times over with the motley hordes and hosts,
That roam in Central America and cut each other's throat's;
Have fought their rebel armies and sunk their pirate boats.
We've cheered for all their Presidents who paid us well in hard,
But would never take their 'paper', or go back on a pard.
We've seen the 'ice blink' of the northern sea, and read by the
   stars of the south,
Been harnessed to an Arctic sledge, and drenched in a tropical
   spout.

IV

We've been blackbird catching for Queensland, taught Russian in
   a Paris school,
And French in the Russian capital, and played as a circus fool;
Been wrecked on the rocks off cannibal coasts and washed half
   dead on the sand,
But always found the cherub aloft could stay the savage hand;
We owe no legiance to King or Prince, but to him we serve for the
   while,
But for him we work with zeal and zest in a bold adventurous
   style;
For we'd cheer for a people's President, or roar ourselves hoarse
   for the Czar,
Sing a song of welcome to peace, or join in a howl for war.

V

Yes! we're a glorious band of Free Rovers, lodged for the nonce
   in Cathay,

Some of us just to stop a gap, others come here to stay;
But we come from all the nations and have known both famine
    and feast,
Can speak all the tongues of Europe and swear in most of the East;
Have fought each other on the continent, settled Californian scores
    with knives,
Stood back to back in China and cudgelled the mob for our lives.
We've friends at all the Legations and relations in the Church
    and 'Beer',
And some of us got our billets by methods uncommonly queer.

VI

All our Clubs are cosmopolitan, though we have our 'ins' and our
    'outs',
With the usual amount of jealousies, exclusions and turned-up
    snouts;
But these pale beside our *cameraderie* when the stones are flying
    around,
And squares are formed to meet the mob or escort the ladies down.
We've been knocked on the head at Mengtsz, burnt clean out at
    Ichang,
Yet never budge an inch from our post for Li, or Chung, or Wang.
When a howling crowd are shouting 'Ta! Ta!' and brandishing
    sticks and knives,
We simply stick our backs to the wall and prepare to sell our lives.

VII

We spend our pay as we get it, for silver goes down by the run,
And if ever we get the kick-out, why we know our way to the fun
To be found at 'the back' in the Colonies: or can ship before the
    mast,
To sail for New York or Liverpool, Glasgow, Cardiff or Belfast.
In our legion we've everyone wanted, from a draftsman down to
    a snob,
Can design or build a bridge or a fort without a cash for the job,
So long as we get our half-pay leave—with a gratuity fat and
    prime—
Then we spread ourselves out in the capitals and have a royal time!

VIII

Our duty's to our liking—though we sometimes grumble at our
    pay
When chasing smugglers across the mountains, or cruising in
    Titan Bay;
We find opium that's stuffed in cats and dogs, and salt that's
    stowed among coal,
Have stiffish fights with pirate junks, see honest ones pay toll;
But we've worn the sombreros of cowboys, ridden in the North-
    Western Police,
And a brush with Indian, Malay, or Pirate, is pretty much all of a
    piece.
Yes! we're Rovers, Free Lancers, Adventurers, call us what you
    darn please,
But we're at home in all the countries, and never at sea on the
    seas.

T. Holman, R.N.

It would be interesting, I thought, to study my fellow members,
and listen to their experiences at first hand. Where better to do this
than at the Customs Club? So, after tea at the Mess, I proceeded to
that establishment and offered a whisky and soda to the Chief Examiner, a genial Scandinavian, with a rich red nose, who knew
how to appraise the quality of liquids. He accepted it with alacrity.

'Skoll', said he as he raised his glass to my health. A ray of sun-
light fell from the window on his rubicund features. I thought what
a good illustration he would make to the lines that strayed into my
mind:

> 'He quaffed his cup of good old sack
> To warm his good old nose!'

'How long have you been in the Customs?' I asked.
'Thirty years,' he replied.
'What were you before you joined up?'
'Able seaman in a tea-clipper.'
'What made you leave the sea?'
'I intervened when the mate was ill-treating a Chinese deck-hand,
and consequently he made my life a hell for me, so one day I took off
my yacket and yumped in the yolly-boat!'

'What do you mean by that?'

'Signed off and went ashore at Shanghai, where I met some old pals in the Chinese Customs, who persuaded me to go in with them, so I applied and was taken on as a Watcher, rising gradually through the ranks of Tidewaiters until I became an Examiner.'

'Can you tell me something of your duties?'

'Funny you should ask that,' he said, 'because I have just been reading a page from the diary of a Customs Examiner, which was actually published in the *Shanghai Mercury*. I have a copy of the paper, so let me present it to you with my compliments.'

I thanked him and took it home for perusal. I thought how lucky I was to have this inside information, and I should like to take this opportunity of expressing my gratitude to author and publisher. I lit my cigar, put my feet on the mantelpiece, and this is what I read:

A PAGE FROM THE DIARY OF AN ASSISTANT CUSTOMS EXAMINER

PART I

8 a.m.: Stepped on toes of Indian watchman, who returned compliment, both trying to sign joint Attendance Book simultaneously. Apologized for being in the way.

9 a.m.: At Wharf Office, Chief Examiner handed me one hundred Import Applications with one hand, while reading morning paper with other.

9.10 a.m.: Climbed one thousand steps to top of go-down in company of one hundred native brokers, bamboo coolies, spies and informers, also one weigher and one scale, invented by Confucius, guaranteed to confuse at point-blank range.

9.15 a.m.: Wiped five gallons of perspiration from brow with old gunny bag.

9.20 a.m.: Swallowed five catties of dust.

9.25 a.m.: Swallowed five million microbes.

9.30 a.m.: Examined bag of black pepper. Junior Assistant's instructions to carefully count and measure contents noted.

9.35 a.m.: Blinded by pepper.

9.40 a.m.: Pushed by party of brokers and fell into cask of molasses.

9.45 a.m.: Pushed by second party of brokers and fell into barrel of coal-tar.

9.50 a.m.: Pushed by third party of brokers and fell into bale of fly cotton.

9.55 a.m.: Tore six new holes in uniform.

10 a.m.: Finished opening, counting, weighing, measuring, classifying and valuing one thousand nailed cases of miscellaneous merchandise.

10.05 a.m.: Showed special ability by slipping on oyster and falling down steps from top of go-down to bottom without breaking anything but record.

10.10 a.m.: Returned to office and pulled C.E. by the whiskers to wake him up.

11.50 a.m.: Finished calculations.

Noon: To tiffin.

PART II

1 p.m.: Returned from tiffin. C.E. handed me one hundred Export Applications with one hand, while trying to keep awake with other.

1.05 p.m.: Proceeded with company previously mentioned to cargo-boats alongside wharf.

1.10 p.m.: Fell off side of cargo-boat into Whangpoo River.

1.20 p.m.: Came up on the other side.

1.25 p.m.: Saved by cargo-stamp thrown in by Weigher.

1.30 p.m.: Weighing beans; slapped bamboo coolie for tipping bag with big toe.

1.35 p.m.: Slapped Weigher for tipping scale with little finger.

1.40 p.m.: Slapped broker for tipping me with squeeze.

1.45 p.m.: Nearly got heart-failure from perceiving Inspector coming aboard cargo-boat in rubber-tyred motor-car. Inspector thoroughly counted all the beans, found one too many and reported case to Peking.

2 p.m.: Finished weighing ten thousand bags of beans and returned to office. Pulled C.E. by the nose to wake him up. C.E. all smiles, reporting I.G. increase of salary of Taels fifty *per mensem* for efficiency and return of seat of breeches from shoemaker, who had them for half-soling.

Said C.E.: 'You do der growling; I ged der ingrease in der shalary! Blease growl some more, ain't it?'

2.30 p.m.: Finished calculations.

2.40 p.m.: Slipped out, patted broker on back and pocketed squeeze, previously refused.

3 p.m.: Paid part of tailor's bill.

4 p.m.: Gave vent to blood-curdling Out-door Staff growl.

5 p.m.: Went to bed with hydrophobia.

GLOSSARY

Native brokers.—Chinese who undertake passing of Customs applications for cargo-owners.

Informers.—A reward, or informant's fee, is paid by the Customs for information leading to detection of smuggling.

Fly cotton.—Waste cotton in bales.

I now began to have some idea of the constitution and general duties of the Service, but I still had my own part to play, and I decided to investigate further into my own responsibilities in order to follow out my mess-mate's injunctions to cultivate a sense of duty, and carry it out effectively, like Edward Lear's naval commander, who treated his crew so well because:

'It was his duty—and he did!'

CHAPTER 3

Civil Servant

There is a kind of wood sorrel which, I believe, is known as the 'Civil Service Plant' from the fact that its flowers open at 10 a.m. and close at 4 p.m. On a dull day, however, they remain closed in slumber all the time.

I was a Civil Servant and it is up to me to prove that the popular misconceptions of general inefficiency and red tape on the part of this type of official are like the prematurely reported death of Mark Twain—i.e. greatly exaggerated.

For I was a special variety of the *genus*. In fact, rather than being a Civil Service Plant I was more of a Sensitive Plant, and I resent any slurs on my capabilities—if any!

It is an interesting fact that, though a British subject, I was an official under Chinese Imperial orders, and a Civil Servant for the convenience of the nations of the whole world. A truly great thought! Of course, the Emperor was not aware of my addition to his Court, but, after all, as he was restricted within the purple walls of the Forbidden City, he knew little of what goes on in the outside world.

If I were an ordinary Chinese official, I should have to put on my ceremonial silk-embroidered robes and bow towards the Imperial Palace in the north every time I received a royal command. As we were receiving new orders and instructions all day long, mostly emanating from Headquarters, I was glad we were not obliged to carry out this ritual!

I had noticed that the Customs Outdoor Staff are provided with smart navy-blue uniforms with brass buttons, but the Indoor Staff were entirely undistinguished in this respect. 'Why this?' I inquired of the Dutchman in charge of the General Office.

'You *can* wear the official Indoor uniform if you like,' he replied. 'It's a beautiful bottle-green with gold epaulettes, and costs a hundred pounds!'

'Where do I get the hundred pounds?'

'Not from *me*!' he said.

'Why are there none to be seen?'

'Probably because none of us has ever been able to save a hundred pounds—except one German Commissioner, who had money of his own. He insisted on the Staff all standing up to attention and saluting when he came to the office!'

I looked at my superior officer's costume. It consisted of a cotton singlet, khaki drill trousers and rope-soled shoes. This was his summer outfit. In the winter he sported a check coat, fur waistcoat, and corduroy breeches. I heard later of a Belgian in charge of a small sub-office who spent the winter in a sleeping-bag and the summer in a bathing-dress! I realized there was no hard-and-fast rule.

Nevertheless it seemed to me that at the outset of my career it was necessary to lay down a definite policy; to make, in point of fact, some good resolutions which should govern my future actions, so that my prospects of success as an executive member of the Customs Service might be assured. Like Walt Disney's third little pig I must build my house of solid bricks. To this end I therefore applied myself.

I have been looking at my original contract or Letter of Appointment as Fourth Assistant, C, which bears my signature witnessed by Mr J. D. Campbell, Non-Resident Secretary, London Office, and E. Bruce Hart (son of Sir Robert Hart). It is autographed at the end by the famous Sir Robert Hart, Inspector-General, and it bears an imposing red circular seal in Chinese characters showing that he is the Agent for the Chinese Imperial Government.

From this the following précis may be extracted:

(1) I must perform all duties assigned to me; (2) I must study the Chinese language, literature, manners and customs; (3) I am employed by the Chinese Government; (4) The I.G. is not liable if salaries are modified or withheld by the Government; (5) I may be discharged for inefficiency after one year, or failure to pass an examination in Chinese in three years, though exceptional ability of other kinds may permit employment in the lower grades; (6) I may be transferred to other ports, promoted, reduced in rank, or dismissed with three months' pay without cause assigned; (7) I may be dismissed without pay for drunkenness, misconduct, or malpractice; (8) I must refund £100 passage allowance if I retire before five years; (9) my retention or advancement depends on Service requirements, vacancies, ability and conduct.

The appointment carried with it a salary of 1,200 Haikwan taels a year. The Haikwan or Custom tael was a fluctuating book currency equivalent then to about a dollar and a half local money, or three shillings. Free quarters were provided.

I gathered from the terms of appointment that, though I could no longer get drunk on Saturday nights, I was given *carte blanche* to be as inefficient as I liked for a year, after which I should have to watch my step. The climate of China does not agree with everybody, so perhaps there will be plenty of vacancies into which I may step from time to time.

My friend in the Mess was of the opinion that the document in question could not be upheld in a court of law, as it really promises nothing definite, but exacts certain definite behaviour from me. In fact, it was quite unilateral.

But I now began to suspect that many Service members, who believed that they were climbing up the ladder too slowly, and had been passed over for promotion 'without cause assigned', were inclined to be rather pessimistic. It seemed to me that the remedy would lie in frankly informing the employee concerned of his shortcomings, of which he may be totally unaware. In later years I always did this to my staff, and they appreciated it, because they were often thus enabled to mend their ways, and render it unnecessary for bad confidential reports to be made on them. I wish I had been treated that way myself. But I am anticipating.

Being still in search of information on which to base my actions, I browsed among the shelves of the office library and tried to read the Circulars issued continually from Headquarters and covering all phases of Customs work and Staff arrangements. I felt like Mrs Partington trying to sweep back the Atlantic waves.

Finally I found what I wanted among some old files of an extinct periodical called *The Rattle*, in the Hankow Club. This production appeared to be somewhat on the lines of *Punch*, and in the issue of August 1896 appeared the following open letter to a Fourth Assistant, B, in the Chinese Imperial Maritime Customs Service of the day. As it is described as an open letter it is presumably available to all concerned.

OPEN LETTER
To a Fourth Assistant, B.

My dear young Friend,

You will, I trust, allow an old resident, one who knew your father in the sixties, to offer you a few words of advice at the outset of your Customs career. I feel that such advice is the more necessary because your father left China twenty years ago, and it will therefore be profitable for you to dispossess your mind, as soon as possible, of any ideas which you may have derived from him concerning your future career and your present surroundings. Similarly I would suggest your forgetting at once everything that you have been told by the amiable gentlemen at the London Office of the I.M.C., especially anything bearing on your Service prospects and the purchasing power of the dollar. For their experience of things Chinese is largely vicarious, and entirely misleading.

I shall not inquire into your reasons for coming to China; you are one of a large family, and the qualifying examination for the Customs must have been child's play to one who failed as easily as you did for Sandhurst. Let it suffice that you are here, and that, since you cannot leave the Service for seven years without refunding your two hundred pounds passage money, you are likely to remain here for ever. For the chance of your possessing two hundred pounds within seven years is quite as hopelessly remote as the prospect of your being fit for any other profession after that period.

Being it so, therefore, let us presume that, in spite of certain disillusions, you are sensibly prepared to make the best of it and to fashion a silk purse out of the material at your disposal. Make up your mind therefore from the start that China is your 'long home', from which only a rich uncle or the Manilla lottery can deliver you. The prospect, however, need not trouble you, for you may observe that those Commissioners who under happier auspices made their piles, now stick closer than ever to their *'otium cum dignitate'*. This, of course, is simply human cussedness, but from it you yourself would probably not be exempt. Also remember that after every five years you are entitled to two years' leave; this thought should sensibly lighten your burdens. But, as it is a hard fact that your half-pay during those two years is calculated to cover your washing and cab-fares only—let me strongly warn you, my young friend, against matrimony. As a single man, you can at a pinch take your leave when due (and enjoy a fraction of existence by sponging on your relatives). But the best of them cannot be expected to put you up if you come bearing four olive-branches and an amah.

These things, however, are in the distance, and you will not remember my advice when they come. Your immediate object, I take it, is to get promotion and a good port; let us therefore review your position and consider the best means you should adopt unto that end. Your position towards the public should go far towards reconciling you to a good many things—for it is unique. The fact is that the public has never known what to make of the Customs, and therefore taking '*omne ignotum pro magnifico*', treats it in a manner very different to the usual 'here's sixpence' attitude with which we associate the word Customs elsewhere. In its first days, of course, the Customs seriously annoyed British merchants of the good old school, and its social position was doubtful in consequence; nowadays, however, and especially since the French war, the pendulum has swung to the other extreme, and your position at most ports will make up for the defects of your pay. There is a good deal in the fact that you may be called upon at any moment to drop blue-pencil and manifests and become an Inspector of Forts, a Naval Commander, an Embassy Attaché, a Postmaster-General, a drill sergeant or a secret agent; and even if none of these things happen to you, their possibility raises you in the public eye. You can, therefore, afford to be fairly independent of public opinion; cultivate, if you like, a certain hauteur and an air of mysterious importance. But avoid truculence in office hours—I know it answers with nine men out of ten; but the tenth may jump the counter and personally assault you.

I should not advise you to become a sinologue; for a sinologue, as the consular and diplomatic records prove, ceases to be an Englishman. Learn, of course, a little Chinese—just sufficient to impress the merchant when he hears you tell the *t'ing-ch'ai* to *ch'ing* the Chief Examiner, or to gain the admiration of your tiffin guests when you tell the boy to *k'ai ch'i shui*. I have known one or two men sustain very scholarly reputations by such judicious use of the language. You have only to run over the names of the Commissioners in the Service List to see that promotion and proficiency in Chinese do not necessarily go together. As to the actual use which the language might be to you, there can, of course, be none until you are a Commissioner, for, till then you will have no relations with the native officials—and if ever you are a Commissioner, you will have nothing further to expect, so can afford to ignore it and the officials, too. Your monthly salary will then be the only thing worth thinking about.

As to office work—avoid zeal of any sort. You can always trust the *t'ing-ch'ai* at any port to know more about its work than you are likely to learn before you are moved to another. Above all do not attempt to master the Treaties and the I.G.'s Circulars; for by the time you have learned them all they will have become obsolete, and then you would have to begin again. Do not worry over Transit Rules or Likin Regulations; nobody understands them (not even the Yamen or the Chamber of Commerce), and if anyone asks you about such things, bluffing is always easy and fairly safe. And you can, if necessary, fall back on 'Port Practice' when cornered.

Keep your eye fixed on Peking and do all you can to get there. It is not a very lively place to live in, and the Fourth Secretary of the Greek Legation will wipe his boots on you; but it is interesting, and it means kudos. Under the eye of the Chief you may not always be comfortable, but you will have acting pay—which is sweet—and the envy of the ports, which is sweeter still. If you should ask what you should do to get called thither, I find it really difficult to say; but all roads lead to Rome. Were you a foreigner, I should advise you to cultivate your Legation and to address *rondeaux* to the Minister's wife; but being a Britisher probably your best course will be to develop some slight eccentricity and learn some kind of wind instrument. Also try to prove that your father went to school in the north of Ireland.

I have reserved my weightiest advice for the last. It is this: Your career and your prospects depend upon your attitude towards Woman—lovely Woman. Impress this fact indelibly on your mind. There are many good hard-working men now vegetating in remote outports whose lives are comparative failures because they never got this advice, or because they neglected it. You remember what our newest poet says:

'Who are the rulers of Ind—to whom shall we bow the knee?
Make your peace with the women, and men shall make you I.G.'

which is absolutely true. Work, worry, luck, languages and lucre, none of these can help you in China as Woman can. Only see that it be the right woman. This is trite advice, and a truth as old as the world; but in China it is one that a wise man will neglect at his peril —and chiefly so if he be an official. As to you, first of all you must bow your knee to your Commissioner's wife; for in her goodwill are comfort and furlough and good sport. But over and above this duty, observe, my young friend, that any women of forty-odd who is willing to smile on your ingenuous youth is worth cultivating; especially if twenty years ago she had a pretty face and an amiable disposition.

Remember that in those twenty years most of your seniors have done their allotted time in Sleepy Hollow and that Mrs Atroy's word has weight with many of them still. One of her little sheets of scented notepaper, delivered at the proper address—be it Legation, Inspectorate, or Princely Hong—may do more for you than many years of blue pencil and honest labour. For men's memories last longer in the easy-going East than we usually give them credit for.

I certainly ought to have kept the advice in the above remarkable document always before me during my career, but I fear when one is young one does not invariably look before one leaps, and the reader will see, in the following pages, whether or not I profited by the recommendations given in the open letter above quoted.

It has been calculated that the average individual spends a third of his life in sleep. As I served in the Customs for thirty-two years, I must have slept at least ten years and eight months—not counting the time I spent in the office! I suppose, however, that I did not sleep much more than the average Civil Servant in any other office.

CHAPTER 4

Head Office

The control of the Customs Staff and the collection and remittance of the revenue was in the hands of the various Commissioners and their staffs in the Treaty Ports, or ports open to foreign trade, some forty in number.

These Commissioners were subordinate to a Head Office known as the Inspectorate-General of Customs, or the 'Royal Family' which for many years operated from Peking, being later moved to Shanghai, and, during the Sino-Japanese War, to Chungking.

The Inspectorate consisted of a number of Secretaries and Assistant Secretaries governing the various branches of the work, headed by the Inspector-General, who was responsible to the Chinese Foreign Office, and later to the Revenue Council.

After payment of staff and office expenditure all over China, and issuing the interest of foreign loans, the balance of the duty collection was handed over to the Chinese Government.

Just as the chief of the Mogul Empire used to be referred to as the Great Mogul, so the Inspector-General of Customs was spoken of, with reverence and bated breath, as the Great I.G. The attribute of greatness particularly applied to Sir Robert Hart, Bart., who was I.G. at the time I joined the Service.

He was an Irishman of considerable ability who was previously in the British Consular Service. His was a master intellect. He served from 1859 to 1911. He was the chief adviser to the throne and had the supreme confidence of the Ministers of the Chinese Board of Foreign Affairs. He negotiated treaties of peace and trade agreements. He was the recipient of about thirty decorations from a variety of different countries, and possessed many literary degrees. He was fond of music and poetry, and was the author of a book called *These from the Land of Sinim*. He did a very great deal to advance the modernization of China, including the establishment of a Postal Service.

It may be of some interest to relate a few anecdotes about this noted man.

An official dispatch was received at a Yangtze port promoting a junior Chinese clerk from the twenty-first of the month. Promotions invariably dating from the first of the month for convenience of accounts, etc., the Commissioner wrote semi-officially to Sir Robert to inquire if it was a mistake. 'No,' the reply came back, 'the twenty-first is correct.' It transpired that the employee in question had formerly served at the Inspectorate in Peking, and the twenty-first was his birthday! This is an instance of the truth of the saying: 'It is always a good thing to have served at the Inspectorate.' The exception often proves the rule, however, and some men have reason to regret that they ever came under such close scrutiny of the Inspector-General. For example, Sir Robert met a young Assistant outside the Chien Men, or South Gate of Peking, and, to test his knowledge of the language, asked him if he could read a Chinese character (*tang*, to pledge), which stood about twelve feet high in heavy black strokes on the whitewashed side of a pawnshop. 'No,' replied the ingenious Assistant, 'I left my spectacles at home!'

Another Assistant was deputed by the I.G. to escort two ladies by train to a place called Ping-An. On their safe arrival the Assistant telegraphed in Chinese '*Tao La Ping An La*', which means 'Arrived at Ping-An', but is also a *jeu de mots* for 'Arrived and peace be with you'. His promotion came rapidly after this.

I also call to mind the French Assistant who obtained three months' leave for the special purpose of taking photographs of everyone in the Customs. I still have a set of those he took of the Shanghai Staff in 1906. They would qualify for the Chamber of Horrors at the London waxwork exhibition. When he had completed his 'Gallery' the results were stuck into a plush-covered album and presented to Sir Robert. He was promoted shortly after. As we told him, his photographs had developed extremely well!

Another British Assistant took a very fine photograph of the I.G. Sir Robert liked it so much that he asked for a dozen copies to send to his friends. The copies were duly presented together with a bill for a hundred taels (about thirteen pounds at the ruling rate of exchange). The bill was paid, but the enterprising photographer was immediately transferred to a small station on a distant frontier, where he languished mournfully for several years!

I wrote to Sir Robert once and asked for a transfer from Kongmoon, a very bad station, to Peking. The reason I gave was that I wished to study the purest Mandarin, or Court dialect, in the capital. He transferred me to Nanking—a most charming spot, with which I was entirely satisfied.

A certain Assistant, who was a European Count, in the days when Counts were two a penny, was transferred from Soochow to Canton, and took three months to do the journey instead of about a week. The Canton Commissioner asked him why he took so long, and he explained that he was invited to stay with various diplomatic and consular officials whom he met *en route*, and he felt it would be detrimental to the prestige of the Service if he refused. The Commissioner reported the matter to the I.G., who was so much amused that he took no disciplinary action at all.

On the other hand, Sir Robert could be very autocratic, and on one occasion he instructed a Commissioner to return—at his own expense—to Chunking from Shanghai, a distance of one thousand, three hundred miles. In those early days the journey took a considerable time and was rather dangerous in a junk through the rapids of the upper Yangtze gorges. The reason for this 'return call' was to enforce the Commissioner to write a trade report on the previous year—an obligation which he had omitted before he left.

My personal contact with Sir Robert was not frequent, but on arrival at my first station I was informed by my Commissioner that the I.G. wished him to inform me that my handwriting was very bad, and that I should go to a stationer's and try various pen-nibs until I found one that suited my writing, and then adopt it for future use. Sir Robert was rather a stickler for good penmanship, though his own calligraphy was very difficult to decipher. As for my own writing, I always got one hundred per cent marks for it in school examinations, but when I signed my contract, or Letter of Appointment, to the Customs Service, I was so excited that my hand trembled slightly when I affixed my sign manual. Hence my first—but not my last—official reprimand.

There is a story told of a certain Russian Assistant to whom Sir Robert wrote:

Dear Mr. ——,

Your handwriting is not all that it should be. One of the essentials to promotion and success in the Customs Service lies in excellent and

clear penmanship. I trust that these remarks will not fall on deaf ears
—long or short.

Yours truly,
Robert Hart.

The Assistant concerned is said to have replied thus:

Dear Sir Robert,
 I have duly received a letter, which, after consultation with experts, I am informed is from yourself. I note your remarks concerning my handwriting, and I shall not fail to profit by them, though there are a few places in your letter, which, due to my stupidity, I find illegible. Should I have been in error as regards your signature, I trust you will pardon me.

Yours truly,
A.B.

This was in the days when there were no typewriters. I believe the first man in the Chinese Customs Service to use a typewriter was a German of the name of Pfankuchen (Pancake); he typed out the Tainan Annual Trade Report for 1893, and it was sent to the Shanghai Statistical Department for printing. This innovation was officially disapproved by Sir Robert, and it was some years before the typewriter was brought into general use in the Service.

I used to wonder what qualities go towards the making of an I.G. Probably organizing ability and the art of arriving at quick and accurate decisions. I have the first to excess, as I always try to organize anything I lay my hands on—much to the annoyance of everybody. But being rather short-sighted, both physically and mentally, I cannot lay claim to being a rapid thinker. I was talking once to the Staff Secretary about one of the Deputy Commissioners.

'He has made very rapid progress in the Service,' I remarked.

'Yes,' he said, 'and do you know why? Because he has an I.G. mind!'

The following interview with Sir Robert was described by Mr Edwin Denby, American Member of Congress, in *The Pacific Era*.

One day in March 1887 the writer, then a boy of seventeen, called upon Sir Robert Hart, Inspector-General of Customs, to ask for an appointment in the Service. The Great I.G. stood, as was his custom, at a high desk in a bleak little office, unadorned save with a few

Chinese scrolls upon the walls. He was enwrapped in a blanket bound about him with a leather strap, which he was accustomed to wear during the cold winters of Peking when at work. Application for appointment in the Service was duly made. Sir Robert said: 'Don't do it; don't bury yourself in China; it is not necessary for you Americans to leave your country and build up careers abroad. We of Great Britain have to; our islands are too small to hold us all, but you have a great, wonderful country. Go home, go to college, and help build up your own United States, and make a career there.'

With the frankness of boyhood I assured Sir Robert that I had no intention of remaining permanently in China, but would retire after my first septennial period of service, and stay at home. Sir Robert said very sadly: 'Ah, no you won't! Many men who come to China think they will go home; home is always a dream, but hardly ever does a man give up service here. There is something in this service that chains us to our tasks. I have known men to resign three times, but always come back again, and take up the old work. If you stay seven years in China, you will live your life here, as I have done; and often, in spite of the great success I have had, and the good I think I have accomplished, I regret, deeply regret, that I did not make my career among my own people, in my own land.'

Three months later I became Fourth Assistant in the Customs Service.

In 1908 Sir Robert went on leave. His health was failing and he knew his life's work was over. Sir Robert Bredon was appointed Acting Inspector-General in his place until 1910, when he resigned and Mr (afterwards Sir) Francis Aglen was appointed Officiating Inspector-General.

In April 1911 I proceeded to England on my first leave and I lost no time in calling on Sir Robert Hart at our London office at 26 Old Queen Street, Westminster. He received me most graciously and apologized for not rising from the sofa on which he was resting. 'Excuse me,' he said, 'for not getting up, but I am beginning to suffer from *Anno Domini*!' He discussed the ports at which I had been stationed, and the Customs men I knew, showed me photographs of groups taken in Peking, etc., and was most agreeable. So interested was I that an hour slipped by unheeded. Reluctantly I bade him farewell. Little did I think it was a final good-bye, for I fully intended to visit him again before my leave expired. However, sad to relate, he died suddenly of a chill three days later. His statue stands in

Shanghai not far from the Custom House. As I looked on it, I thought
of the old Latin tag:

'*Si monumentum vis circumspice!*'

Sir Francis Aglen received the substantive post of Inspector-
General in 1911 after the death of Sir Robert Hart. I had the honour
of working under him in the Chinese Department of the Inspectorate,
one of the duties I performed being a translation into Chinese of a
pension scheme for the Service, which was approved of by the Government. Sir Francis was very kind and considerate to me, and his wife,
Lady Aglen, was good to my wife and family. I found him to be
energetic, just, and ever ready to give credit where credit was due.
Though a practical man, he had his aesthetic side. He was extremely
gratified when the ex-Emperor conferred upon him the order of the
Yellow Jacket, which entitled him to ride in the Forbidden City.
Strangely enough he was keenly interested in psychic phenomena,
and, during his visits to England, he never failed to attend the meetings of the Psychic Research Society. I remember once, when he was
dining at our house, he told us that he had actually seen an example
of levitation, when a man was hypnotized, and, in a state of trance,
rose from a recumbent position and floated slowly out of an upstairs
window and into one on the ground floor! When he left the Service
in January 1927, I was at Tientsin, so I went to the railway station
to say good-bye to him as he passed through. He died a few years
later, so he has now solved the problem of the spirit world. *Requiescat
in pace*.

Mr A. H. F. Edwardes was then appointed Officiating Inspector-
General. I had worked at the clearance desk in the Shanghai office
with him in the early days. I called on him at Peking and congratulated him on his good fortune. As I looked at him I thought to
myself, 'There, but for the grace of God, goes Charles Williams!'
He retained his position for about a year, which is probably more
than I would have done! He was a good linguist, and was gifted with
charm of manner and real ability. He resigned in 1928.

But the Chinese Government, chafing at treaty restrictions, now
required an Inspector-General who would press for a large increase
of tariff and other reforms, and decided that Mr (afterwards Sir)
F. W. Maze would be a suitable representative, though formerly it
had been the practice for the new I.G. to be nominated by his predecessor. Mr Maze told me that he had been approached in this
matter even as early as 1926, when I saw him in Shanghai, where he

was then Commissioner. He hesitated at first, but eventually accepted, and took over the Inspectorate from 1929, though previous to that time he held the position of Deputy Inspector-General.

Sir Frederick Maze did much to improve general staff conditions, and during his tenure of office the tariff was fully revised, and many useful publications were issued. He held the Service together, and steered the ship of State through some difficult times—including the Sino-Japanese War. He was arrested at Shanghai by the Japanese and confined for some time in a cell measuring ten by twelve feet, together with about eighteen other persons—British, American, Russian, and Chinese. Sanitation was primitive. He and his fellow prisoners endured great privations, and, in some cases, torture. They were made to sit cross-legged on the floor without any support for the back, and were only given one bowl of rice-congee and four slices of bread each morning and some tea in the afternoon. Finally he obtained his release, and left China, but made his way later to Chungking, the new capital, where a new Head Office was eventually formed.

Again I thought of the saying, 'It is always a good thing to have served at the Inspectorate.' But life was certainly less complicated when *I* was there!

CHAPTER 5

Imperial Glories

The Empress Dowager Tz'u Hsi, who held the reins of government at the time I went out to China, was known as the 'Old Buddah' —a tribute to her great power.

During the Boxer rising in 1900 she had been very much afraid that her throne was in danger from the so-called King of Peace, the head of the rebels, and, being very superstitious, she was actually inclined to believe that the Boxers had the spiritual powers of invulnerability, etc., to which they laid claim. She therefore decided to divert their activities away from herself and towards the foreigner.

She authorized the issue of an Imperial Edict to all Chinese provincial officials to exterminate all foreigners in the country, and ordered the Boxers to attack the foreign Legations at Peking. It was a policy of desperation.

As is well known, many foreigners were killed, and much property damaged and destroyed but the siege of the Legations ended in the defeat of the Boxers by international relief forces, the net result being the destruction of the pride of China, the Summer Palace at Yuan Ming Yuan, and the infliction of heavy indemnities. The Hanlin Academy was situated next to the Legation Quarter, so it was set on fire by the Boxers in the hope that the flames would spread to those buildings, a calamity which was averted by the defenders; its invaluable library of Chinese books thus perished.

As the allied forces advanced towards the Forbidden City the Emperor, Empress, and other members of the Imperial household and some Court officials, left all their possessions and fled incontinently far into the interior of China.

On her return the Empress Dowager consoled herself with the thought that she had saved the Dynasty from the Boxers, and, in order to save her face, she built herself a new summer palace out of certain funds which had been set aside for the formation of a navy.

When I was stationed at Peking as a member of what was often facetiously called the 'Royal Family', i.e. the Inspectorate Staff, I met a Miss Carl, who was an artist, and the sister of a former American Commissioner of Customs. The Empress Dowager had decided to invite Miss Carl to paint her portrait, which she intended to present to Queen Victoria, so, in spite of the fact that her friends advised her not to risk going alone to the Forbidden City, yet she did so and painted the portrait.

The Emperor Kwang Hsü continued to be held confined in the Forbidden City, and affairs of state conducted by the Empress Dowager until 1906, when, one day, I opened my morning paper and was astonished to read that they had both died suddenly and simultaneously, for some unknown reason!

On the death of the Emperor the child P'u Yi came to the throne with the dynastic title of Hsüan T'ung, his father Prince Ch'un acting as Regent. The Republican Revolution occurred in 1911, and the Ex-Emperor P'u Yi was then kept a prisoner in the Forbidden City, just as British sovereigns have been held in the past in the Tower of London. The Imperial dignity was preserved for some time without the Imperial power, but in 1917 he was restored to the throne for twelve days as a result of a rising in his favour. Sir Reginald Johnston, formerly Governor of Weihaiwei, was his tutor, and educated the boy along British lines. P'u Yi adopted the name of Henry, from his favourite character Henry VIII, and he named his wife Elizabeth after the great Queen. Sir Reginald tried, without success, to persuade the British Minister to extend the protection of the Union Jack to Henry P'u Yi when Peking was invaded by General Feng Yü-hsiang in 1924, but finally the Japanese Minister took him under his wing, and he remained a pawn in the hands of the Japanese Government for many years! He was taken to Tientsin, where I had the honour of being presented to him and his consort in 1926 at a dinner given by the Japanese Consul, and later at a reception in his honour at the British Consulate. He had a slight, stooping figure, with an intelligent face and high forehead, and was wearing large tortoiseshell-rimmed spectacles. He conversed at dinner chiefly about Chinese art. At the British Consulate reception he suddenly disappeared, but was found later out in the garden sitting on a rustic seat in the moonlight, and writing a poem, which he afterwards presented to the Consul. The poem drew comparisons between the beautiful colours of the ladies' dresses in the ballroom and the variegated hues of butterflies' wings.

Shortly after that time, with Japanese assistance, he became installed in Manchuria under the title of Emperor Kang Te (Tranquillity and Virtue), and resumed the worship of Heaven and the use of the Dragon as an Imperial emblem. He finally lost his throne, for the third and last time, at the end of the Sino-Japanese War, when Manchuria reverted to China.

After the Japanese surrender the Ex-Emperor was captured in Manchuria by the Russians, who carried him off to Moscow as a political prisoner. His ill-fated consort, the Empress, made her way back to Peking, the original scene of her former splendour. I heard, in 1948, that she was living there with her two sons in such reduced circumstances that she had been obliged to sell some of the Imperial jewellery in order to provide the necessary means of existence!

The old Imperial palaces and throne rooms of the Forbidden City are of great beauty and interest. They are truly magnificent and stately edifices, on high marble terraces, their gay-coloured roof-tiles agleam in the bright sunshine, showing up in sharp contrast to the masses of shadow in the surrounding courtyards, paved with wide stone slabs and decorated with large bronze figures of birds and animals. In the old days they were exclusively reserved for the use of the Imperial household and a few privileged guests, and were rigorously forbidden to the common people. They are now thrown open to the public, who are admitted on payment of a small fee.

I have had the honour of examining the bed on which the Emperor Kwang Hsü died, and I have seen and handled the thrones occupied by him and other Emperors before him. I have been many times to the Forbidden City, and have studied its beautiful treasures of jewels, porcelain, jade, etc., before they were removed to Shanghai during the Sino-Japanese disturbances in 1933. Some of these treasures were conveyed to England in June 1935 by H.M.S. *Suffolk*, for display in the Chinese Art Exhibition at Burlington House, London.

The Emperors of China were laid to rest (often later disturbed) in spacious tombs approached by avenues of colossal stone statues of warriors, officials, and animals. As these statues are in pairs, they rather put one in mind of the Noah family and their menagerie, and, after all, why not? For, according to Chinese tradition, a Great Flood occurred in the province of Shansi, when all were drowned but one man and woman, who escaped by riding on two tigers, which carried them to the top of Jen-tsu Shan, or 'Mountain of Man's Ancestors'.

They did not return 'with smiles on the faces of the tigers', but lived happily ever afterwards and became the parents of the human race. I have made several visits to the Imperial *mausolea* outside Peking and Nanking cities, where I often noticed women throwing stones on to the backs of the sculptured elephants. The reason, I was told, was a superstitious belief that if the stone did not fall off the woman's next child would be a son.

Enormous sums were spent on the Royal funerals, and there are many recorded instances in China's history where numbers of women and servants, together with animals, were killed and buried with their Royal master, together with the workmen who knew the secrets of the construction of the tomb.

The Royal deceased was attired in his Court dress, and profusely adorned with jade, pearls, and other gems of great price. Numberless gold and jade ornaments, and showers of pearls, to the reputed value of over six million sterling, were poured into the coffin of the Empress Dowager, and a quantity of porcelain, pictures, bronze and silver, were placed in the vault. The following description of these was given in an article by Mr Moore Bennet in the *Illustrated London News*:

The treasures buried with the Empress Dowager were tabulated at the time by the notorious eunuch Li Lien-ying as follows: 'A mattress seven inches thick, embroidered with pearls, lay on the top of the coffin, and on the top of it was a silk embroidered coverlet strewn with a layer of pearls. The body rested on a lace sheet, with a figure of Buddha woven in pearls. At the head was placed a jade ornament carved into leaves. She was dressed in ceremonial clothes done in gold thread, and over that an embroidered jacket with a rope of pearls, while another rope of pearls encircled her body nine times, and eighteen pearl images of Buddha were laid in her arms. All the above were private gifts, sent by friends. Her body was covered by a sacred Tolo pall, a chaplet of pearls was placed upon her head, and by her side were laid 108 gold, jade and carved gem Buddhas. On each side of the feet were placed one water-melon and two sweet melons of jade, and 200 gems made in the shape of peaches, pears, apricots and dates. By her left side was placed a jade cut like a lotus-root with leaves and flowers sprouting from the top: on the right hand was a coral tree. The interstices were filled with scattered pearls and gems, until the whole spread level, and over all was spread a network covering of pearls. As the lid was being lifted to place in position, a Princess of the Imperial house added a fine jade ornament of eighteen Buddhas and another of eight galloping horses.'

Unfortunately, in 1923 the tomb of the Empress Dowager was opened and pillaged by undisciplined soldiery after the battle of Kalgan during the civil war between the rival Generals Wu Pei-fu, Feng Yü-hsiang, and Chang Tso-lin!

Some of the pearls eventually found their way to the Peking market. I saw one of the necklaces. The pearls were quite black after being buried in the royal sepulchre for fourteen years. But where lies the dust of their owner? Floating hither and thither, and perchance mingled with the breezes gently wafted over the Imperial palaces, lakes, and gardens. *Sic transit gloria mundi!*

CHAPTER 6

Shanghaied

Many of the members of the Outdoor Staff of the Chinese Customs were recruited from the ranks of those that 'go down to the sea in ships', and, in their early days, very likely may have been 'shanghaied' before they actually came to Shanghai. Be that as it may, I have been 'shanghaied' myself.

By this I do not suggest that I have been drugged and shipped before the mast, though as a matter of fact I was once placed under guard and taken to Shanghai in a semiconscious condition.

This was because I was laid low with paratyphoid in Nanking, and the missionary doctor there had filled me up with pills of different colours which only seemed to make me worse. He told me to take a pill of a certain colour at a certain time, and one of another colour an hour later and so on; I did my best but I felt rather colour-blind at the time! In the end my Commissioner had me taken down by train to Shanghai in charge of an Examiner.

There I was put into the General Hospital, and given the French ice-water treatment for three weeks, which consisted in wrapping me in a sheet and letting me down into a cold bath filled with lumps of ice. Being entirely unnerved by this torture, I was brought round with a glass of champagne!

The purpose of this was to reduce my temperature. It did. I soon dropped below normal, but fortunately they took me out before I went below zero. I enjoyed the champagne—though I should have preferred it without ice.

Part of the treatment was gradual starvation. I begged for food, but it was refused. One day a friend came to see me and suggested that I should watch my opportunity and slip across the road to the hotel and have a good dinner with him. I did so and was discharged from the hospital the next day. The nurses were surprised at my sudden recovery, but, of course, it was due to the nourishing hotel food, which they knew nothing about. Discussing this case with a doctor one day, he said I was kept without food because it was necessary for me to grow a new coat to my inside, as the other one was worn out. By eating solid food I ran a serious risk of perforation of the gizzard. However, all was well and my withers remained entirely unwrung!

Apart from this adventure, I was 'shanghaied' on two other occasions. I mean that I was appointed to Shanghai once in 1905 for eighteen months and again in 1916 for three years and four months.

It was interesting to compare the conditions in Shanghai on my second visit as a married man, after a lapse of ten years, with those I experienced on the previous occasion as a bachelor.

In the early days a motor car was seldom seen, open carriages being the order of the day. I felt extremely grand when I hired a Victoria, and went bowling along the Bubbling Well Road behind a spanking pony, a nicely-drawing cigar of great size jutting at a jaunty angle from the corner of my mouth, and a sense of *bien aise* gently radiating throughout the whole of my being. Cigars were cheap in halcyon days of only five per cent duty. Moreover, had I not been early informed that a cigar is a *sine qua non*, or essential feature? As I puffed the fragrant weed into the sunshine, my youthful spirits soared. It was glorious to be alive; it was delightful being in China, and it was exciting to have a job in which I was keenly interested. As I looked around me, I could echo the sentiments of the Chinese student who wrote of Shanghai:

The vasted land which was far away from the settlement before has been covered by magnificent buildings which are used up to be general stores and the goods therein are beautifully displayed through the big glass windows. We will notice also that the people walking on the streets are so neatly dressed that it seems they are shameful to meet the beautiful street if they are dirty.

Shanghai, *lit.*: 'Approaching the Sea', was originally a muddy waste intersected by dikes and canals. It was formally opened to foreign trade in 1843, and the various concessions were gradually developed until a settlement of great importance came into being. The country is flat and productive of fair crops. There are fine recreation grounds and gardens; also a good racecourse. The Chinese city was surrounded by a wall in my time, and contained a market and some temples; and a tea-house with an artistic bridge, which is said to be the origin of the design of the willow-pattern chinaware.

In 1915 I occupied a flat in Shanghai with my wife and family, situated over the offices of the *North China Daily News*, and nearly next door to the old Custom House, whose clock struck the hours and quarters almost as loudly as Big Ben. The sounds of the road traffic, the bells of the trams, car hooters playing tunes, ship sirens on the river, etc., were heard by day, and at night the printing machinery on the floor below continually vibrated like the screw of a steamer. At five a.m. every morning a crowd of Chinese ragamuffins arrived cheerfully singing and whistling, while queuing up for their bundles of daily papers for sale to the public. The trees along the bund were full of rooks usually cawing vociferously at the same time, and their numbers were occasionally reduced by shooting.

Needless to say, in the midst of this *brou-haha*, I never overslept myself and had no excuse to be late for the office, but it was quite a relief when we moved out to a vacant Service house in Hart Terrace, where all was peace and quiet again.

Some years later, when I was in charge of the Ningpo office, my wife and I received an invitation from the Shanghai Customs authorities to witness the ceremony, which we duly attended, of the laying of the foundation-stone of a new Custom House at Shanghai. This building was on the site of the old one, and, as may be seen from the illustration of the architect's design, is a very fine piece of work and forms a striking landmark on the foreshore. It contains a lift and many new departments, and is a great improvement on the former office.

When the guns were booming in Europe and World War One was under way, there was a call for volunteers for active service. Though I was prepared to offer my services as an interpreter for the Chinese Labour Corps, it was decided that it would be inadvisable for too many British subjects to leave the Customs. So I was not to be 'shanghaied' out of Shanghai. Nevertheless, I was impressed into the service of the Shanghai Volunteer Corps, in which there were a number of companies of different nationalities, and took my turn to guard the British Consulate and other public buildings at night. During the early part of the war, the German Volunteers still continued in Shanghai, and, on full parade days, were quite conspicuously doing the goose-step in the public recreation ground along with all the rest of us (doing other steps), but finally they were disbanded, and all German subjects—including those of the Customs Staff—were repatriated to their native land. My Company was the Customs Company, a regular 'Legion of Far Cathay' as poetically depicted earlier in this book, and we were sixty strong.

I cannot say that my experience shows that I am cut out to be a brilliant soldier, but this is chiefly due to my weak eyesight. Curiously enough, though I could never hit a stationary target, I often secured a knock-out blow on what was known as 'the moving man'—a figure representing the upper part of a soldier which rose unaccountably from a trench and then went back again. Possibly I visualized him as a passing pheasant.

I remember once being on guard at the British Consulate, where I spent the night in full uniform in the Consul-General's office with my head on his large Chinese dictionary. Suddenly we were called out by our commanding officer and ordered to present arms for inspection. Being half asleep, one of my comrades absent-mindedly pressed the trigger of his rifle and the bullet just missed my left ear and struck the ceiling, from which a shower of plaster fell on our astonished heads! My ear often tingles now at the memory of this incident, as it also does when I think of the bad shot made at the rifle range by a Chinese soldier, who nearly turned me into cold mutton. Occasionally we bivouacked in the Customs Club, where a friend of mine went comfortably to bed one night on a billiard table. The Club Secretary was very wrathful and threatened to charge him so much an hour for monopolizing the table in this rather unusual manner!

Alexander Graham Bell, a native of Edinburgh resident in Boston, U.S.A., was experimenting in 1876 with a view to devising some method of improving the weak hearing of his fiancée, when he hit upon the reproduction of the voice by electricity. This led to the invention of the telephone. Engaged couples have found it very useful ever since, but it has its drawbacks as well. At Shanghai I had a telephone installed in my house, and every few minutes it rang and a Chinese inquired '*Sa ni ga?*' (Who is there?) only to find that he had the wrong number. This is due to the fact that there is a certain similarity in the Chinese sounds of some of the numbers, such as ten and four, etc., and because the Chinese invariably shouts loudly and incoherently into the phone because he knows his voice has a long way to go. After a time I invariably replied that I was the *Dalai Lama of Tibet*. This generally eased them off! But our telephone number was one which had lately been used by a French gentleman called Blanc, who had evidently been very popular (or notorious) before he

Hong Kong at Night

Lightning on the Whangpoo River, Shanghai, 1917

(*Night photograph by the Author*)

New Custom House - Shanghai

left Shanghai. I stopped this eventually by declaring, 'Non, Monsieur Blanc est *mort!*'

There was no telephone in my office, but my wife occasionally rang up the Chief Tidesurveyor's Office, from which a message could be given to me in an emergency. One day she rang up and asked, 'Is that the Tidesurveyor's Office?' 'No,' was the reply in a very beery voice, 'there ain't no tides comin' in 'ere!'

One day a Russian gentleman knocked at the door and asked permission to use the telephone. The house-boy admitted him and left him in the hall with the instrument. The gentleman left the house after a while—with the telephone receiver and my best overcoat! Moreover, in the pocket of my overcoat was a letter of my wife's which I had forgotten to post. This was, of course, very serious for me!

It is easier to live on credit in China than in any other country in the world because of the chit system. You may sign a chit, an IOU, or an order on one's compradore (business manager, from Portuguese *compra*, to command), for almost anything. It is most convenient and economical until the end of the month or quarter, when large bunches of these chits are presented to you for payment. A well-known emporium, or general store, caught fire at Shanghai when I was there, and all the firm's outstanding chits were burnt—much to the delight of the customers. However the firm delivered accounts to all those who were suspected of owing money, and, in one instance, on a chance, sent out a bill for a saddle to a dozen possible purchasers, when, strange to say, *eleven* people paid the bill. The only one of the twelve who refrained from settlement was the actual purchaser! There was also an Irish lady who had overdrawn her bank account, so she merely wrote a chit for the amount due, and sent it, with apologies for not having arranged the matter before!

I was having breakfast at the old Palace Hotel one winter's morning in 1903, on my first visit to Shanghai, when I noticed an elderly gentleman with long white hair at the next table. He seemed to be fairly bubbling over with good humour and was laughing and chatting with his table companions. This was only natural, because his name was Samuel Clemens, better known as Mark Twain. On his stay in China he was very much interested in the old pilots of the China Coast, as he himself was once a pilot on the Mississippi River. Perhaps some of these old pilots had been 'shanghaied' in the days of their youth. In any case, they had good stories to tell of their China experiences. But Mark Twain could 'beat them to it'—as they say in the United States—and he was certainly 'no slouch' at spinning a good yarn himself!

Shanghai has passed through many vicissitudes since those early days, and life there was not always all beer and skittles. In 1937, for instance, bombs were suddenly dropped one day from the air for no reason at all on Avenue Edward VII and the Nanking Road, killing about 1,300 and wounding some 360 innocent civilians. Curiously enough the planes which dropped these bombs were Chinese, it being supposed that they were either aiming at the Japanese flagship *Idzuma* or else the pilots were wounded and the bomb-racks damaged. After this came the destruction of the Shanghai suberb of Chapei by Japanese aircraft, and the fighting became general. A number of foreign houses were hit by stray bullets, including my old flat over the *North China Daily News* office. I am very glad I was elsewhere at the time, and no longer a 'Shanghailander'!

CHAPTER 7

Customs Declarations

'Have you anything to declare?' asked the Customs officer. 'Nothing,' was the classic reply of Oscar Wilde, 'except my genius!' An American Commissioner, retiring from the Chinese Customs Service, on return to his native land, was asked by the New York Customs to open his luggage for examination. He opened a trunk, and, on the inside of the lid, in large capitals, were the words: 'MR. —— COMMISSIONER OF CUSTOMS.' The Customs man, on reading the inscription, merely said, as he closed the box, 'O.K., Chief. *Shark don't eat shark!*' Personal effects of Legation and Customs officials are usually accorded duty-free treatment. I was having my luggage examined once on arrival in England on leave, and remarked that I was in the Chinese Customs. 'How are they doing out there?' asked the Examiner. 'You have two pounds ten to pay on these cigars!' Then he turned to a lady waiting in the queue, who looked remarkably stout, and said, 'If that's lace you have wrapped round under your clothes, you needn't have troubled. The duty was taken off last month!' Such a man should go far.

It is strange how everyone considers Excise and Customs duties are levied for the primary purpose of being evaded. Even Adam Smith, the noted political economist, regarded smuggling as 'a crime which Nature never meant it to be'. One nautical gentleman was so angry when I called upon him to pay tonnage dues before his ship would be allowed to clear that he went purple in the face. I offered him a cigar, which calmed him down at once. Here again I realized the important function of the cigar in Customs practice, and I have often used it in similar cases. I think I should have been justified in entering it under petty cash as regular office expenditure. Commissioners in the larger ports are provided with entertaining allowances, which, after all, is much the same sort of thing.

In the Shanghai office, a very noisy place, commonly known as the

Monkey House, the Customs declaration comes into its own, and is visible in thousands, all piled up on the large flat desks, while on the other side of the long counter are a cosmopolitan crowd of applicants all talking at once in many different languages—a regular Tower of Babel!

During my first year in Shanghai I laboured at the export and clearance desks, and then at the 'wrong file' desk. This latter was inaugurated in order to explain to applicants the mistakes they had made on their forms. I had some lively times explaining some of the mistakes, many of which were due to ignorance, but others made deliberately to defraud the revenue.

The Shanghai re-export desk was in charge of a rather eccentric individual (now gathered to his fathers). He possessed three hundred and sixty-six ties, one for every day, including Leap Year. He was a regular encyclopaedia of knowledge, and would go round the office putting down five cents on each desk, and propounding a general question, which, if answered correctly, entitled the one addressed to the five cents. Nobody could solve any of his problems. However, one day we had an idea. We looked up a number of difficult subjects in the library at the Club, and made out a question for each person in the office. One by one we fired our questions at the gentleman concerned, who was unable to answer any of them. After that he discontinued his practice of asking further questions himself.

There is a Service rule that Assistants should be moved to a new desk every three months. This is to ensure that they acquire a thorough knowledge of the complete routine of the office. This rule is not always strictly carried out, however, so I invariably applied for a transfer to another department four times a year, so that I could complete my experience. There were no fixed working hours. At some desks we had to work very late, at others the hours were more regular. The two most interesting were the wrong file desk, as above mentioned, and the memo desk, where all duty was calculated.

I am afraid I was not very popular with the Deputy Commissioner in charge, as very likely it was not always convenient to move us about. Eventually he got rid of me altogether by appointing me to the Post Office to take charge of a new department there for collection of duty on postal parcels, a very important work in Shanghai, as more duty is collected on Shanghai parcels than on ordinary cargo at most other ports.

Once I took over the wharfage dues desk from a Continental

gentleman (who shall be nameless). When handing over the account-books, which were very untidy, he said, 'If you make a mistake it doesn't matter. The paper is very thick, so you can easily rub it out!' He then proceeded on leave of absence without a care in his heart. I found it impossible to make head or tail of these accounts, which were practically illegible because of the multifarious alterations. I was obliged to take all the applications for the last three months and examine them again, in my own time after office hours, to find the mistakes. Then people began to inquire as to the whereabouts of my predecessor, who owed money right and left, several thousand dollars. As a matter of fact, he never came back from his leave, and so I suppose he effaced himself as well as his clerical errors! Anyhow, he was gazetted as 'Disappeared'.

The office-boys of the Custom Houses were very efficient, and, though their pay was low, they had responsible work in sorting and stamping all the duty applications. One Shanghai office-boy of about 1896 was said to have been so honest and capable that he eventually became a Postal Commissioner! At present most of the office-boys have been replaced by responsible clerks.

Of course, we had some queer 'customers' to placate. I have heard as many excuses and grumbles as any Customs official living, but I think the man who most nearly succeeded in convincing me of the righteousness of his cause was a well-known conjurer and illusionist on the English stage. When theatrical properties were imported into China the owner had to pay wharfage dues (a small charge for the upkeep of wharves), and a deposit of money, the latter being refundable on re-exportation. This London entertainer came to the office with an application on which he had declared the importation of his 'illusions'. He protested against the payment of wharfage dues and deposit, because, he explained, 'Although these are theatrical properties, I can make them disappear at any time by simply waving my magic wand, so strictly speaking, they don't exist at all! How then can you charge me on something that has no existence?'

The clearance desk work was especially uninteresting, and consisted in the checking of innumerable applications with cargo certificates (a system which, I am glad to say, has since been abolished), and initialling them with blue pencil. This we did all and every day, often until seven o'clock at night.

One very fat French Assistant who was unable to keep awake,

trained himself to initial in his sleep. The office-boy would bring a large pile of applications, which he would initial blindly and automatically. Some evil genius obtained a number of applications from the wrong file desk, containing mistakes, and pushed them under his pile. These he also initialled and passed as correct, and, consequently they were brought back to him by angry persons from various desks one after the other throughout the day. He certainly became quite awake for a time!

As may easily be imagined, we used up a great many blue pencils at this desk. One day a memorandum came down from the Stationery Office upstairs stating that the number of pencils used was unusually high, and asking for an explanation in the interests of economy. The masterly reply was sent back: 'We have so much work to do that we all get very hungry, and so we often feel obliged to *eat* the pencils!' I believe the air was quite blue in the Stationery Office, as the Assistant in charge there, a German known as 'Old Thunder and Lightning', was noted for the shortness of his temper.

As one had to initial so much in the office, it was natural that we tried to reduce the strokes of the initial to the simplest possible form. Consequently many initials were undecipherable, and, moreover, quite undistinguishable from one another. Finally it was decided by the 'powers that be' that, in future, initials should not be made to resemble snakes, straight lines, or indeterminate curlicues. It is, of course, a well-known fact that signatures are often entirely illegible. Instead of typing a letter and writing the signature, it would really be better to reverse the process. There is now a rule to the effect that the name must be typed in brackets after the signature in official correspondence. Apropos is a story of Lord Curzon, when he was Governor-General of India. Having waded laboriously through numbers of badly written reports, he finally made a minute on the dossier: 'I agree with the views of the gentleman whose signature resembles a trombone!'

Routine work becomes deadly in its awful monotony, and it often helps if a little comic relief is occasionally available.

One day an applicant came to the public counter of the re-export desk and asked to see the Assistant in charge. He wore a very bushy red beard and his manner was swaggering. 'I am an opium grower from Ireland,' he said, 'and I have a large shipment of several tons of Irish opium for distribution in different parts of China. If you will kindly help me to pass this contraband through the Customs I am willing to pay you a good commission!' The Assistant in charge became very excited, and sent for the Chief Tidesurveyor, the Chief Examiner, and several Tidewaiters to investigate this flagrant case of smuggling. Then the pseudo-applicant pulled off his false beard and revealed himself as one of our regular office colleagues!

In those early days new inventions were being introduced into offices and homes every month or so. The world, after a long sleep, was entering into its busy mechanical age. When I first went to Shanghai there were punkahs in the office, as there still are in some of the smaller stations. When electricity began to come into general use it was decided to install electric fans instead. A number of desk fans accordingly made their appearance. The first day they were put into operation several hundred applications became entangled in the blades and were torn to ribbons. After that ceiling fans were established. But we never quite extricated ourselves from the chaos of that first electrical innovation. It created quite a furore, but for once the 'powers that be' were at fault. So we were happy.

The brains of the Shanghai office were undoubtedly assembled at the memo desk, where duty was assessed. We had various nationalities there, British, American, French, Spanish, Norwegian, and Japanese. I got very much interested in piece goods there, and made a collection of classified samples in a card index. I obtained permission to attend a series of lectures on piece goods which was delivered to the Customs Examination Staff by our piece goods expert, who had been recruited from Manchester. He was a burly North Country man with a sense of humour. 'Let me impress upon you,' said he one day, 'that reps, ribs and cords have nothing whatever to do with the rope that Haman hung himself with!' He was rather bald, and remarked, 'Look at my head and remember that Kemps are dead fibres,' He graphically described the 'Devil'—a machine with large teeth, which chewed up old clothes and converted them into shoddy for cheap apparel. It was an amusing game to guess the name of each sample handed round for inspection and classify it as animal or vegetable.

I am of an inquiring turn of mind, and, like Rosa Dartle, always asking for information, so I was anxious to trace the Customs application from its source, and I was allowed to study its treatment outside the office and in the examination sheds.

Let me return to the general office. One day I was moved to the re-export desk, which was under the control of the gentleman with the three hundred and sixty-six ties. I was early on arrival in the morning, but soon my superior officer came striding in. He was a tall, well-set-up man, with a long narrow face framed with locks of hair hanging down on each side over his ears, and slightly curled at the ends. His moustache was pointed and shaped like the handle-bars of a bicycle and he wore a short imperial beard. His eyebrows were high and well marked, lending a slightly quizzical or inquiring look to his face. His fingernails were long and sharply pointed, and he had very small feet shod in high-heeled shoes. He hung up his large brown sombrero hat. His tie (probably No. two hundred and fifty-two) was of purple embroidered velvet secured with a gold ring under the knot. The coat was cut in at the waist and the trousers bell-bottomed. He wore a dark brown otter-skin waistcoat.

He sat down and I wished him 'Good morning'. He lit his pipe, which was a strange contrivance with a glass bowl in the centre. As he smoked the nicotine collected in the bowl and began to boil and bubble exactly like the coffee in a percolator. So, of course, I lit my cigar. Unfortunately the charm did not work. He was very annoyed. He pointed to a tobacco-jar in the centre of the desk. 'Everybody at this desk,' he said sternly, 'has to smoke my tobacco.' I had no pipe, so he immediately presented me with one of his. I filled it with his tobacco, which was a blend of his own, and was apparently Turkish with a strong flavour of nutmeg. I suffered no ill effects from the tobacco, but unfortunately I swallowed the liquid by mistake instead of emptying it out into the spittoon as he did! Finally I mastered the necessary technique and all was well.

The work of the re-export desk consisted chiefly in verifying the particulars of original importation and issuing drawbacks of duty. It seemed to me that giving back good money was rather bad business, and we ought, at least, to charge something for the time and trouble of calculation. I very soon found that lots of people tried to claim refund of duty on goods they had never imported at all. In such cases fines were inflicted or the goods confiscated, according to the seriousness of the offence. After all, the Customs is not a charitable institution!

At the end of the day my Chief invited me to a cocktail-party. I thought it would be good policy to accept this kind invitation, so I duly presented myself at his address, and was introduced to his young son of fifteen, and instructed to take him on at ju-jitsu! I obeyed and was soon laid flat on my back by the young savage! I decided to take lessons for purposes of self-defence in future. A good champagne cocktail soon restored me to semi-consciousness. The boy and his father then played to us, the former on the bugle, and the latter on an organ which was fitted with various extraneous gadgets, such as bells, drums, etc.; the effect was quite impressive in a piece called 'The Battle of Trafalgar'.

My host then opened up a steel cabinet and showed us his collection of uncut gems, which were certainly very beautiful, especially one which took on different colours according to the strength of the light. I think he said it was called a 'jargon'—but these lapidary terms are all Greek to me.

He had a marvellous contrivance for keeping himself cool at night. It consisted of an endless band of flannel, which passed through a tank of ice-water under the bed, and then over the pillow, travelling just a few inches above his face. It was operated by clockwork. I rather wished I had one myself when the nights were so very hot. But I wonder what would happen if the mechanism went wrong in the middle of the night, in which case perhaps I might be strangled in my sleep with ice-cold flannel! I shiver to think of it!

But this seems to be a far cry from our Customs declarations. Instead of cooling our·noses, let us put them to the grindstone!

CHAPTER 8

The Art of Smuggling

In order to avoid the Customs tariff, a vast system of smuggling has been introduced all over the world. On an average, some ten thousand seizures of tobacco, cigars, spirits, and drugs, etc., are made annually in the waters round Great Britain, while the application in the Straits Settlement of the rubber restriction scheme (designed to enhance the price) led to a certain amount of smuggling by dealers who were anxious to exceed their quota. There has been a considerable amount of bootlegging (originally concealing in the sea-boots) of wines, etc., into America. In fact, smuggling is universal, and there are even special organizations in many parts of the world for the packing and delivery of all kinds of dutiable and contraband articles, concealed as other goods paying little or no duty, which are distributed—for a consideration—to any port required.

China, with its lengthy and indented sea-coast, offers great opportunity to smugglers, who do not hesitate to take advantage thereof. However, the Chinese Maritime Customs is capable of checking the activities of smugglers to some extent by means of its Preventive Department, with a well-organized fleet of Revenue vessels continually patrolling in Chinese waters; while searching-parties board vessels in order to investigate all possible 'hides', or hiding-places, in which dutiable or contraband goods may be concealed.

There are hundreds of different ways of smuggling; for example, goods may be concealed in various steamers, on the person, in luggage, in boxes and baskets with double tops, bottoms or sides, in wash-tubs with hollow sides, in false bottoms of clocks, lamps, teapots, jars, in bundles of books with cut-out spaces, in furniture, etc. Arms and ammunition are smuggled in pianos, beer-barrels, machinery, etc. Opium is found in double-bottomed trays and cooking-pans; in bamboo carrying poles; between the inside and outside of native hats, in cloth tubes woven into carpets, in picture frames, in socks, belts, blankets, clothing, in oranges, bread, soap, candles, as kernels in groundnuts, worn as false calves of the leg, etc. It has even been found in a box full of live snakes. Various drugs are discovered in the oil-boxes of railway trains and lavatories on steamers, and the centres of millstones and bean-cakes.

A bottle of cocaine may be concealed in the watch-pocket of a man's trousers. Hashish, the extract of hemp, may be placed in the double bottom of a basket of fruit. A piece of hair may be clipped out of a camel's coat and the package of morphia inserted and affixed with glue, after which the hair is stuck on again; or a false lump may serve as a convenient receptacle. Heroin, a derivative of opium, may also be concealed in the hollow tubes of brass or iron bedsteads.

Pigs, disguised as human infants, have been known to be smuggled across the frontier, certain women having resorted profitably to the scheme of dressing up their pigs as their own babies. At first stupefying the animal with a swig of alcohol, they were able to avoid a telltale squeak when passing over the border with the 'sleeping child!' And a man with a glass eye has been found guilty of smuggling diamonds in the interior of that artificial organ.

Goods have been disclosed in oil-tins, hollow bricks, sweet potatoes, silk cocoons, pigs' bladders, and wooden tubs of wine, sauce, etc., the liquid being contained in a separate section with a bung tap.

Automatic pistols have been found concealed in the false bottoms of bird-cages, or mixed with other goods. A few years ago a number of electric flash-lamps in the shape of a revolver were imported into China; they sold like wild fire because they were bought in large quantities by the bandits infesting the province of Chekiang, who used them for the purpose of holding up the ignorant villagers and relieving them of their surplus cash! These articles are now classed as dummy weapons and their importation is prohibited.

Opium and other harmful drugs are found hidden in coal-cubicles, in coal-trucks, in the steel piping of railway cars, in the double roofs of carriages, behind panels in trains, in ventilators, among car springs, in brakes, in watertight bags in the water tanks, in window frames. Morphia arrives from abroad in various chemical combinations, in sugar or milk, in saccharine, in soda; a book arrives by post entitled 'The Inculcation of Moral Practices', its heart filled with the drug. The Customs often seizes shipments of patent medicines with a large content of harmful drugs, already having on file a list of

some fifty varieties bearing names such as 'Dragon's Spittle Anti-
opium Pills', 'Civilized Pills', 'Anti-opium Pills for Youthful People',
'Might and Prosperity Pills', 'Dr Yale's Brain Stimulant Remedy',
cough lozenges, asthma and colic cures.

A steamer arrives from London with a large compartment
constructed in one of its coal-bunkers containing about 3,000 lb of
opium, the only immediate access to it being through a manplate in
the stokehold plastered over with cement, through the bilges and up
through the bottom of the bunker. A shipment of 2,700 cases of
'water softener' is discovered at Shanghai to have concealed in it
nearly 4 tons of opium, which, if it had not been found, would have
realized a profit of over $1,000,000 on an initial outlay of about
$150,000. An innocent-looking Japanese rug is seen to have the warp
made of paper cylinders filled with opium. A sedate Chinese gentleman carries a bird-cage, with a bird gaily singing in it, the false cage
bottom being filled with the drug. A motor-launch on the West
River has a false bottom in the oil-tank. Soldiers in the Tonkin
border carry opium in false haversacks. Pedlars along the country
paths carry opium mixed in soot and blacking in their hats, in match-
boxes with a layer of matches on top, in hollow rolls of silk and cloth,
in dummy candles. An old Chinese woman boards a steamer at
Canton with a basket containing a cat with five newly-born kittens;
the mother is very solicitous of their welfare even though they are
dead and stuffed with opium!

There is no end to human ingenuity and nothing new under the
sun. Sir Robert Hart, former Inspector-General of Customs, was the
unsuspecting victim of an opium smuggler who concealed opium in
his luggage on board a Customs cruiser. The same trick was tried on
Sir Francis Aglen, who succeeded him.

A common method of clandestine importation is to throw overboard a case of smuggled goods attached to a buoy or an anchor, and
at some subsequent time the articles will be brought ashore by a
small boat which has been waiting for such opportunities.

Hides on vessels are usually destroyed by the Customs. These may
be either natural or specially constructed in different parts of the ship.
These hides are numerous and varied, and new ones are continually
being devised. The main principle is that anything hollow is liable to
suspicion. The term 'hide' is used to express the idea of a space or
enclosure on board any ship (or vehicle), which conveys to the
Customs the impression that it has been specially devised for the

purpose of smuggling or concealing goods, or has been constructed or adapted from any part of the permanent structure thereof, or of the movable equipment thereon, or of any attachment thereto, and covers such additional sections as bulkheads, false bows, double sides, double bottoms, etc., which could be used for the concealment of goods.

Natural hides on vessels have been discovered in store-rooms, cabins, bulkheads, water-tanks, boilers, coal-bunkers, engine-rooms, water-pipes, galley-stoves, water-closets, chain-lockers, bilge-pipes, etc., and specially constructed hides in roofing, deck-planks, stairs, furniture, tool-boxes, hollow hatch-coamings, etc.

When found, such smuggled goods are confiscated, and if the offender is found as well, he may be sent to the law courts for punishment according to the seriousness of the offence. False declarations of ordinary merchandise, i.e. declaring high quality to be low, or false declarations of quantity, weight or value, with intent to defraud the Customs, are wilful contraventions of the regulations, and punishable by fine or confiscation. Confiscated goods are sold by auction, resold to the owner, or, as in the case of drugs, destroyed or presented to hospitals.

I was a member of the International Anti-Opium Association at Peking in 1920, and was present at one of its meetings when Sir Francis Aglen, Inspector-General of Customs, made an interesting address on the subject of the Chinese Customs Service and the prevention of illicit trade in opium, morphia and kindred drugs. He drew attention to the various loopholes open to the smuggler, namely: (1) unguarded land and sea frontiers; (2) foreign concessions; (3) railways; (4) shops; (5) abuse of the parcel post; (6) leased territory; (7) foreign harbours; (8) native production of opium (9) opposition by officials. And he pressed for the support of the Chinese Government in controlling these loopholes.

There is an old Chinese saying, 'So long as there is opium there will be no revolutions' (*yen pu ssu—chu pu luan*). What it says is no doubt true, but the national use of opium to the extent implied leads to a peace that spells national death and annihilation in the present age of political and economic competition. The Customs does its best to discourage the smuggling of opium, etc., but, alas! revolution in China appears to be a chronic disease for which no satisfactory remedy has yet been discovered.

CHAPTER 9

Sleepy Hollow

Sleepy Hollow is, I believe, a peaceful valley on the Hudson River, where the old Dutch settlers grew enormous cabbages and blissfully smoked their large porcelain pipes in the shade of the weeping willow trees.

Its counterparts exist in many examples elsewhere, especially in China, and I knew it would be my fate to spend part of my life therein. Therefore when, towards the end of 1906, I was transferred from the busy metropolis of Shanghai to the newly opened outport of Kongmoon, I was not surprised. 'Good-bye to civilization,' said the Chief Accountant, as he handed me my travelling expenses. Though I replied airily, 'Civilization only cramps my style!' I really felt rather depressed.

Kongmoon city proper is situated three miles up a small creek debouching from the West River, and its chief industries, I was informed, were silk, pewter, groundnut oil, and palm-leaf fans.

I acquainted myself with my duties as Secretary and Accountant, and then I explored my new home with some curiosity. As my eye roamed over the expansive rice-fields and mulberry patches, I noted how differently the fields were arranged compared with those in the north. What impressed me more than anything else was the fact that there were so many dikes. Obviously Kongmoon was accustomed to floods. In the centre of the largest field there was a goose-herd with a long bamboo pole, talking to his flock in a succession of short guttural sounds, which the geese appeared to understand perfectly. He was in the act of driving them towards the small mat-shed in which they would shelter for the night. I learned afterwards that these goose-herds are far more practical concerning the welfare of their birds than they are about themselves. He may sleep under a tree, but the geese must have a house so that they may remain healthy and grow fat for the market. It seems to be a recognized fact among the geese that the last one in gets beaten with a bamboo pole, so they all hurry as fast as they can!

The goose-herd seemed rather to resent my idle curiosity and shouted at me from the other side of a small stream, 'Kong Ye So Fan Kwai!' I have a good ear for sound, and the next day I asked one of the office clerks what this meant. It was, literally, 'Speak Jesus Foreign Devil', or Missionary! Such was my welcome to Sleepy Hollow!

From time to time I made expeditions in the surrounding country-side, sometimes crossing the river to an island where I made friends with the caretaker of a large orchard of lichee and orange trees, who allowed me to eat as much fruit as I liked for twenty cents (about two-pence). On other occasions I climbed some of the low hills in quest of the 'chikor' or red-legged partridge, a very difficult fellow to shoot.

I made a visit of inspection to a groundnut factory. The nuts, mostly imported from the neighbourhood of Canton, were piled up in sacks against the walls of a large store-room. Everything was managed in a primitive though effective and inexpensive manner, the very peanut shells being used for fuel in each of the four brick stoves, upon which were roasting the nuts previously crushed into a powder. To each stove was assigned four men. One man was merely the stoker, and was engaged in throwing large handfuls of husks into the hole at the side of the stove. Another, the cook, was kneading the mass of nut-powder with his hands in a steel cooking-pan shaped like a washing-basin. Now and then he flung out portions on a mat spread out on the ground. On the mat was squatting a man, naked but for a piece of rag round his waist. His business was to heap together the powder, or more properly pulp, in a bamboo ring, fold the mat over it, dance about vigorously on the top in his bare feet, remove the ring, and lo and behold out came a groundnut-cake resembling an enormous biscuit, which he handed to another equally thinly clad individual to dance upon a little more in his turn. Finally he placed it on the growing heap of cakes to cool. The cakes, when cool and dry, were stuffed into a hollowed tree-trunk, and pressed from both ends with blocks of wood, which were screwed in by hand until the oil ran out of the compressed mass in a thin stream into a wooden receptacle. The cakes are sold to other enterprising persons, who contrive to extract yet a little more oil out of them, and then sell them to be finally used as fertilizer for the crops. This is a typical example of the widely prevailing system in China of utilizing all waste products to the fullest extent. The oil is used in cooking, lighting, soap-making, and lubrication.

My next discovery was a silk filature establishment. This consisted of a large go-down or shed, inside which were sitting long rows of young girls. In the middle of the shed was a steam motor which supplied the power for rotating a number of square wooden frames. On these the silk was being wound off from the cocoons by the working girls, who earned thirty to fifty cents a day. The cocoons were placed in round pans of warm water, and deftly manipulated with chopsticks. The girls were very handy in picking up a thread here, a thread there, with their chopsticks, and joining one thread to another so that it ran off smoothly without interruption. The smell of stale cocoons permeated the air. There is no smell quite so horrible. Yet the workers are allowed to eat these cocoons, which they actually enjoy!

I now remembered the advice, given to me at the outset of my career, to cultivate the goodwill of my Commissioner's wife in Sleepy Hollow. When I arrived I found my chief was unmarried. Apparently the only woman he had ever loved was the late Edna May, so celebrated as the Belle of New York, and her photograph was in every room of his bungalow. After a time he was transferred elsewhere. I cannot help regretting that he never married Edna May! He was replaced by a Portuguese with a wife and two daughters, who were all very kind to me. They even bought me a new hat, because they said my old one was not fit to be seen! We had many good picnic parties on the Customs launch, when proceeding on visits of inspection along the river.

On a hot afternoon I sometimes used to stroll to the top of a hillock in the Customs compound, and stretch myself out at full length on the soft grass, and survey the scene below. The creek, a shimmering ribbon, wound itself in and out among the low rolling hills, and sluggishly washed the shores of various small islands which here and there impeded its course. In the immediate foreground was a garden, cultivated with great care, for it was a source of income to its owner. As I watched one day a man approached to make a purchase of potted plants. In one part of the garden a peasant girl, her jet-black hair in a plait finished off with red silk cord, was drawing from a well two wooden buckets of water, and, having cooled her parched face in one of them, she proceeded with her double burden, affixed to a bamboo pole, to the house of her master. In another

Temple of the Emperors and Kings at Peking

(Photos by the Author)

Roofs of the Summer Palace

corner two masons were engaged in building an artificial rockery with rough pieces of blue granite in the midst of a small lake planted thickly with pink lotus flowers.

Each day seemed the same in Kongmoon. The eight white men, of whom I was one, soon exhausted their curiosity about each other, and waited—there was little else to do but work and wait—until the powers that be should see fit to transfer us to another more lively station.

After office business was concluded I used to sit on the hill and watch the two steamers *Taion* and *Takhing* as they got under way for their twelve-hour journey to Hong Kong. Then I would slowly rise, and as I did so three or four pigeons, startled, would dart out from near by, and wing their way rapidly to a small clump of trees, where they roosted for the night.

And now the peaks of the distant hills were lit up with small bonfires, not for destructive purposes, but so that the ashes of the burnt brushwood might be washed down by the rains to fertilize the fields in the plains below. The pawnshops were closing their doors. They were tall square towers, with a massive door at the bottom barricaded with strong poles to keep the contents from the possible assaults of marauders and pirates, who occasionally made raids on the district.

Sometimes I applied for a day or two's leave of absence, and I once travelled to Canton and paid a visit to the Temple of the five hundred Lohan (Disciples of Buddha). They were drawn up in vast array, 'pride in their port, defiance in their eyes'. The highly coloured image of one of these worthies had what seemed to be a bowler hat on. 'Who is that?' I asked the custodian, who was hovering around in the hope of a *cumshaw* (tip). 'Marco Polo,' he said. 'Ah yes, and who was he?' I inquired. 'He was a *Frenchman!*' was the astonishing reply. Such is fame! As a matter of strict fact, I found out later that it was really a figure of Dharma Pala, an Indian priest of the sixth century, and not Marco Polo at all!

In the summer of 1908, I was sleeping on the roof of my Chinese house (no foreign buildings had then been constructed) when suddenly a heavy typhoon arose and blew away my mosquito-net, so I went down inside and spent the rest of the night on the dining-room table. In the morning there was a flood and I hailed a sampan (rowing-boat), which came right into the house to the foot of the stairs, and boarding it I went through my own front door to the office!

I watched the first Kongmoon Custom House being built (it has now been replaced by another). It was situated on the river bank, and constructed of grey bricks on a raised foundation to avoid floods. There was a veranda on the ground floor and on the upper floor.

While at the Kongmoon office, besides my regular work, I also compiled an Anglo-Chinese Glossary of Customs Terms, which was printed and included in all Customs Office Libraries throughout the whole country. It went into a second edition, but is now, naturally, out of date. However, I hope it was of some assistance at the time in Customs translation work.

My next move, at my own request, was to Nanking, an interesting town surrounded by a high brick wall, on which one was able to walk. I had comfortable quarters and there was excellent shooting. Again I served as Secretary and Accountant, and I also had charge of the Postal Accounts and moneys. Here I was privileged to witness the ceremony of the worship of Confucius, which was held just before daybreak in the large Confucian temple, and attended by all the Chinese officials in their beautiful embroidered robes of state.

Nanking, which is situated on the Yangtze River, was not of great importance when I was there, though it had been an Imperial capital in the past. However, it again became a capital after I left and was developed along modern lines until it passed into the hands of the Japanese, who treated the place rather badly. Now it is back again in Chinese control.

The first President of China, Dr Sun Yat Sen, was buried just outside the city of Nanking in an elaborate mausoleum of granite and marble. No expense was spared in its construction. Passing through a triumphal arch, a road edged with cypress trees leads to a terrace and pavilion containing a memorial stone 30 feet high. Here begins a flight of 224 steps to the mausoleum. In the central hall is a white marble statue of the great patriot, and on the walls his political testament and other texts are engraved. Huge bronze doors lead from the hall to the domed burial chamber, with floor and walls entirely of the purest white marble.

'Ningpo More Far', as it is commonly called, in reference to its out-of-the way position up the Yung River in the province of Chekiang, arouses mixed feelings in my mind as I look back to my strange experiences at this distant outpost. I was stationed there twice, first in 1912, when I arrived back from home leave with my bride and we set up house very happily on the river bank, though we had to move out of it soon after to give place of honour to a senior Japanese Assistant (whom I had known in Hankow). We had a houseboat provided by the Service for picnics into the country, which was most beautiful. On the second occasion, 1925, though I was no longer a junior Assistant, but Acting Commissioner, and living in the largest house, for the first time I was unhappy, for reasons which I will now relate.

In that year a Chinese employee was killed in a strike at Shanghai connected with a Japanese mill. The students espoused the cause of the strikers, and at the same time resented certain new by-laws of the Shanghai Municipal Council, one of which was the enforced registration of printers to prevent the dissemination of seditious literature. The demonstrators threatened the jail, and the police considered it necessary to fire on them, most of those who were shot being natives of Ningpo, who were brought back there for burial. This gave rise to a feeling of great unrest, not only at Ningpo but all over the coastal provinces.

There was a boycott of British trade in Hong Kong and three hundred thousand strikers left the island for Canton, where they paraded along the bund near the foreign settlement of Shameen just across the narrow canal. A shot was fired by some person unknown, which led to a rifle and machine-gun fusillade, and caused about two hundred Chinese and some twenty foreign casualties.

Gradually the movement developed a Communistic tendency and finally became chiefly anti-Japanese. This was rather unfortunate for China, because the Japanese very soon found a pretext for making war on China on a large scale, and much suffering ensued. Gradually the enthusiasm of the strikers weakened and many of them enlisted in the army.

Nobody would have thought, a few days before, that in a proverbially quiet Sleepy Hollow like Ningpo, whose very name, literally 'Peaceful Waves', seemed to indicate continual tranquillity, that any troubling of the waters would be likely to occur. But a howling mob broke into the house of a Japanese Customs Assistant on my staff, removed the furniture and burned it on the bank of the river, and broke up the woodwork of the interior with iron bars. This furniture was the property of the Chinese Customs, but the rioters thought it was Japanese. There was a Russian Assistant also living in the same house, and they both escaped at the back.

The British Consul and I reported the matter to the local Chinese authorities, who eventually made some arrests, but feeling was very high, and the men were soon released, as they declared that they had seen the Japanese Assistant ill-treating a Chinese rickshaw coolie. I was unable, myself, to obtain any definite proof of this, and the Chinese Government accepted the sworn declarations to be authentic, which, of course, placed me in a very unenviable position, being— apparently—unable to control my own staff! And this unfortunate and unexpected incident, over which I had no control, led to my being removed for transfer elsewhere!

Our little Ningpo riot provided very startling headlines in the London papers: 'NINGPO IN FLAMES! CUSTOM HOUSE BURNT TO THE GROUND!' etc., and I received frantic telegrams from relatives in England inquiring as to the safety of myself and my family. To the accompaniment of crackling fire and crashing glass we got the children out of bed, and my wife took them by boat upriver, with other residents, to the Asiatic Petroleum Company's installation, where they spent the night. One of my small sons remarked, 'It's a great pity they're burning up all those nice tables and chairs!' I waited until Chinese soldiers arrived, but no other houses were attacked.

I began to think that Sleepy Hollow was a name no longer applicable to some Chinese outports, and that the sooner I got away, far away, from 'Ningpo More Far' the better! Before leaving, however, my wife and I had the honour of dining on Admiral Sir Edwin Alexander Sinclair's yacht, which came to Ningpo with the late H.R.H. Prince George, Duke of Kent, who was on board as a lieutenant. The British Consul also gave a tiffin in honour of the Prince. My wife sat next to him at the dinner on board, and he told her he was interested in China and the customs of the people. The naval party paid a visit to the graves of numerous British soldiers who gave their lives in the defence of Ningpo against the Taiping Rebels in 1861. The Admiral heard that my daughter had been asking to go on board, so he gave a special children's party, which was duly attended by all the youngsters. Our smallest boy climbed up on a big gun on deck and was rescued by Prince George just as he was about to fall overboard!

Among other good instances of Sleepy Hollow may be mentioned Kiukiang and Wenchow. I had a year at Kiukiang, a small port on the Yangtze at the foot of the Kuling Hills. I was in charge of the general office at my previous port, but when I reported to my

Kiukiang Commissioner, a very pro-German Baltic Russian, he said he was sorry to see me because he had applied for a German Assistant, as he considered the Germans were so much more efficient than the British; and this being so he put me in joint charge of the general office with a Chinese clerk—an indignity which I think it would be hard to beat! However, I turned out to be not so bad after all, as I managed to close certain loopholes where duty had been evaded—perhaps by previous German Assistants—for many years past.

The Custom House was pulled down and rebuilt while I was there. I suggested that it would be more healthy to move into a vacant building until the new Custom House was ready, but my Chief was using that building as a curio museum and picture-gallery, and insisted on our remaining during the process of reconstruction. The result was, of course, that most of us suffered from throat trouble owing to the dust and germs from the foundations, and half the staff went off duty sick!

My quarters were also under repair, being riddled with white ants, but eventually, after this rather bad start, I settled down comfortably with my family. In the summer we occupied a delightful bungalow in the hills, and I went up and down in a sedan chair to the office every day; by the side of the bungalow was a cascade flowing into a bathing-pool.

I have happy memories of Wenchow ('Genial Region'), which is situated up the Ou River in Chekiang, for it was the first port where I was put in charge as Acting Commissioner. It is a most beautiful spot, being a walled city surrounded by ranges of wooded hills, which certainly rival, if they do not surpass, those in the Scottish Highlands.

During the three years I spent here with my wife, three children and their governess, in a large house with a beautiful garden, I began to feel myself something of a veteran in the Service. I was able to carry out various improvements to Customs property, and to revise the working of the Native Customs, which collected taxation on inland goods. I was made a Director of the Famine Relief Bureau, and helped in the raising of funds for relief of distress in the surrounding district.

Commissioners are supposed to eschew politics, but sometimes they are unavoidably drawn into them. This happened in 1924, during the Kiangsu-Chekiang civil war, when the city of Wenchow was occupied by the victorious troops of the Kiangsu General, Sun Chuan-fang, under the command of Brigadier General Peng Techuan.

All the inhabitants fled. Wenchow was like a city of the dead. The local officials took refuge in foreign houses, and I was required to take charge of some of their personal effects.

A number of foreign gunboats soon made their appearance, the first to arrive being the French sloop *Algol*, which landed armed men to protect the French Mission. Capitaine d'Hervieux of the *Algol* requested me to go with him to visit the chief Chinese civil official, the Taoyin, and act as his interpreter. He wished to notify him that as the representative of the French Government he would patrol the city and maintain peace and order, seeing that there were no police for that purpose. I found it rather difficult to speak French and Chinese and think in English at the same time, but I managed it somehow! The Taoyin washed his hands of the whole business and said he was sick and going into hospital at once—a common case of political indisposition. Gradually the situation eased down as the weather improved. I have often noticed that disturbances in China are always worse in the summer, when the people have what they call 'Jo Hsin'—or 'hot hearts'. But on the arrival of the autumn cooler judgements prevail.

The first house I ever owned was at Wenchow. I bought an acre and a half of rocky land on the hills there for seventy-five dollars (about six pounds), but the Chinese authorities told me that I was only entitled to the 'skin of the land, and not the bones'. This meant that I was not allowed to extract minerals and take them away. They had no objection, however, to my using the rock as building material for the house. I engaged coolies to prise out the beautiful blue granite outcrop with crowbars and shape it into square blocks, with which I built a very useful summer bungalow with a flat roof for two thousand dollars (one hundred and sixty pounds). It had two bedrooms and a sitting-room, and servants' quarters behind. I sold it to the Methodist Mission at cost price when I left, after using it for three summers. It was very pleasant to go up in a carrying-chair every afternoon, bathe in a mountain pool, and have supper on the roof far above the twinkling lights of the city.

Another purchase, also sold when I left, was a sailing-houseboat, which I found most useful for picnic and shooting trips. On one expedition we sailed down river to the foot of a picturesque mountain, with a creek running under a stone bridge at one side, and a flight of stone steps leading up the hill, which was covered with pine, fir, maple and other trees, with here and there the dark grey lichenous rocks showing through the foliage. There were six hundred steps up to a temple known as Yang Fu Ssu, or the Temple of the Sun Palace, dedicated to the God of Thunder. We walked up the steps, obtaining a fine view of the surrounding country. In the plain below were fields of bright green crops interspersed with little villages. In the distance stretched the mountain ranges, the highest point of which is named Hart Peak after Sir Robert Hart. The temple contained idols and models of junks presented by local fishermen to propitiate the gods and ensure good catches.

We had a terrible typhoon at Wenchow, which removed half the corrugated iron roofing of our quarters, and torrential rain came down the stairs like the Niagara Falls! The iron sheets were blown off the roof to a distance of three or four hundred yards, and for several days were being brought back by little Chinese boys, who were asking a dollar each for them. The next morning we noticed that every roof in the city had suffered similar damage!

Looking back on my experiences, I can only conclude that Sleepy Hollow may be inclined to be inherently sleepy, but, nevertheless, I kept my weather eye open there all the time!

CHAPTER 10

Along the Coast

'We are having a rough passage,' I remarked to the skipper of a small Chinese coasting steamer ploughing its way heavily through an angry sea.

'Well,' he said, biting off a piece from his plug of tobacco, 'You see that calendar hanging on the bulkhead. When it sways from side to side I know there's a bit of a swell on. But if it makes a complete revolution, then I reckon it's really rough!'

I have made many a journey round the China coast, and, though I have never seen a calendar loop the loop, yet I have certainly struck some dirty weather, especially in the typhoon season.

And, of course, the smell of the deck cargo is not always conducive to a peaceful frame of mind. I remember one particular trip from Wenchow to Ningpo, when the cargo consisted of live pigs in crates and dead eels in tubs! And on a voyage from Hong Kong to Tientsin on a coal-boat we became thoroughly begrimed with coal-dust, which we inhaled in our sleep and ate with our meals! It was everywhere!

In August 1905, I made a very enjoyable trip from Shanghai to the Saddle Islands and back. Leaving at 12.30 p.m. on Saturday, in company with some forty or fifty passengers, on S.S. *Lita*, we arrived at our destination about 9 p.m. and found ourselves in a sequestered bay formed by the arms of the largest island in the group. At six o'clock the following morning I went ashore by sampan with a few others to a beautiful stretch of sandy beach, where we undressed and enjoyed a delightful bathe.

A rather curious incident occurred here. While I was swimming my gold ring fell from my finger. I saw it glitter as it dropped through the water, and plunged after it, but failed to recover it. When I came up to the surface again I noticed a good-sized fish flapping about, with a piece bitten out of its back, probably by some larger fish, and so I took it ashore. I cut the fish open, and, when I looked inside I found—absolutely *nothing*!

Here is another true fish story. On the way by launch, some years later, from Chefoo to Lungkow, on the north coast, I opened a tin of peaches for lunch, and threw the empty tin overboard, where it was immediately swallowed by a shark. I wonder how it agreed with him!

It was in the summer of 1917 that I went to Chefoo for a holiday, where the bathing was excellent. The Williams pear has been grafted on the local variety with great success.

I went on to Lungkow, a sub-station of Chefoo, to stay with an old friend of mine who was in charge of the Customs at that place. We had some shooting and fishing along the shore, and one day we sailed across the harbour in a gig and visited a lighthouse on the headland. It was very hot, so we spent the night in the open air on camp beds, though the revolving light was not exactly conducive to sleep. In the morning our mosquito-nets were entirely covered with centipedes, moths and other insects apparently attracted by the light!

I have visited Swatow, on the coast of Kuangtung. It is a healthy place, but often suffers from violent typhoons. The Customs are on the mainland, but the Consulate and most foreign houses are on Kakchioh island a mile away.

Amoy is another interesting and beautiful port on the coast of Fukien. The foreign settlement is on the island of Kulangsu, where some extraordinary volcanic rock formations are to be seen. One of these rocks weighed many tons and was balanced on another one, but could be made to rotate and swing from side to side with a touch of the hand. A party of sailors from a foreign gunboat, on shore leave, succeeded in dislodging this rock, which had been there for centuries, and rolling it down a steep cliff into the sea, much to the disapproval of the natives, who looked upon it as sacred!

I have landed at Tsung-ming Island and other islands in the Yangtze delta, for purposes of shooting. The reed-beds are full of pheasant, while numerous water-fowl abound in the marshes.

Of the many islands in the Chusan Archipelago, near Ningpo, Pootoo is the most famous, being entirely devoted to Buddhist worship on account of the tradition that Kuan Yin, the Goddess of Mercy, made a divine appearance there in A.D. 847, and lived in a cave on the island for nine years. I counted nearly a hundred monasteries and temples there besides a pagoda and various sacred rocks with carved inscriptions. A brisk trade is carried on by the priests in 'Passports to Heaven', which they are willing to write out and sell to all comers at $300 each, or more if you think it is worth it. Unfortunately I could not even run to $300! The name Pootoo is derived from Mount Pataloka in the Buddhist Paradise, which is the present address of the Goddess of Mercy.

Of all the islands I have visited the most beautiful is Hong Kong, and I have paid visits of inspection to various Customs stations on other islands in the neighbouring waters. Never have I seen such powdery white sand and such a number of variegated shells of all colours and shapes.

I was appointed Deputy Commissioner in the Kowloon office situated in Hong Kong in the spring of 1927 after a year's leave in England. My wife came with me, but our children remained behind at school. My new duties consisted chiefly in controlling the revenue collection and work of the various sub-offices on the land and water frontiers, and I was also appointed Examiner in Mandarin for Hong Kong University. I was in temporary charge for a time, when I compiled a memorandum on the work and reorganized the office arrangements.

Hong Kong is very picturesque from every aspect. Here one is in a position to recall the vision of:

'Magic casements opening on the foam
Of perilous seas, in faery lands forlorn.'

The island of Hong Kong, *lit.*: 'Sweet Lagoons', was originally a mere fishing-village on a barren rock, with five thousand inhabitants. It was the haunt of smugglers and pirates, and the Emperor is said to have laughed heartily when he handed it over to the British in 1841. When the British came, the pirates transferred their activities to Bias Bay. Owing to the consequent immunity from bandits and kidnappers, the natives have poured into the colony in vast numbers, where they live happily in peace and security under British rule. In my time there were 640,000 Chinese residents! There was also a boat population in the harbour amounting to some 70,000, who are very exclusive, and will not intermarry with the land-dwellers. The British inhabitants only numbered 8,000.

The town slopes backwards at an angle of twenty-three degrees. The Peak is 1,825 feet above sea-level, and is reached by cable tramcar or motor road. The island is eleven miles long, and from two to five miles broad; the circumference is about twenty-seven miles.

On the mainland across the harbour lies the Leased Territory of Kowloon ('Nine Dragons'). It was leased to Great Britain in 1860 and 1898, and has an area of 280 square miles, including also the small islands of Lantao, Lamma, Cheungchow, etc.

Gazing down from our house on the Peak to the harbour below, with its glittering lights, was like looking into the window of the largest jewellery establishment in the West End of London. Repulse Bay is the Hong Kong Lido, with its hotel and neat rows of bathing-huts. The Hong Kong harbour is one of the largest in the world, and is ever thronged with vessels arriving daily from the Seven Seas, laden with all manner of merchandise. Ores from Malaysia, hard-wood from Borneo, rice from Indo-China and Siam, hemp from India, charcoal from Chinampo, tin from Singapore, sugar and paraffin from Java, wine and soap from Marseilles, spirits from Glasgow, potash from Djibouti, gypsum from New York, dyes from Hamburg, all unloaded at Hong Kong and China ports in exchange for local and Chinese produce of all kinds. The bum-boat women busily ply their sampans and slipper-boats. Junks, with their broad lateen sails, float ponderously hither and thither. One never tires of watching this interesting kaleidoscope.

But it was not always so peaceful. These halcyon days were rudely interrupted by the Japanese when they seized the island during the war, but now the British are back in control again. But difficulties occasionally arise with such a large Chinese population. Owing to overcrowding in the Leased Territories and the eviction of Chinese squatters from condemned buildings there was serious trouble in 1947, resulting in rioting directed against the British Consulate in Canton.

From Hong Kong, I went up north to Tientsin, which is the largest port on the coast above Shanghai. It is situated in Chihli at the junction of the River Pai Ho and the Grand Canal. Goods are transported from here to Peking by train or cart. Evaporation of salt is an important industry. There are public gardens and a fine racecourse. The country is not very fertile owing to the soda in the soil.

I served here as Deputy Commissioner for a year, but found the work rather uninteresting, as it consisted chiefly in supervision of others, with little or no opportunity of doing anything constructively useful on my own account. The Commissioner went on holiday to Weihaiwei in the summer, and I was placed in temporary charge.

The local Quarantine Service was in need of funds, so I obtained a grant from the Chinese Government through the Superintendent of Customs to ensure its proper functioning in the future. I bought a good second-hand Ford car, which was useful for inspection of wharves and examination sheds, and for going to the Recreation Club for tennis, swimming, and dancing. I sold this car for cost price when I left.

I often used to call on the gunboats when they visited port, and I met with much hospitality from naval officers, whom I invited in my turn to tennis parties, and I also took them out shooting and for picnics in the country by launch or houseboat. Sometimes we dined on board, and often a concert was given by the ship's crew. One evening I was dining on an American battleship. After the soup the second course consisted of small pies. I cut into the pastry and found inside a wad of cotton wool held together with a rubber band. Investigating further into this *pâté au surprise*, I found a folded paper on which was drawn a very clever sketch of a Custom House officer extracting money from a Chinese merchant held firmly in an iron press, which, by *peine forte et dure*, gradually squeezed him so that all his dollars emerged from his mouth. Under this was the following suggestive inscription:

> Dear Williams, you'll pardon us, please,
> We've heard of the Custom House squeeze.
> Pray accept this small token
> 'Tis better drawn than spoken—
> And then you can work with ease!

Other guests were served with similar confections. The sketches were made by the ship's surgeon, and the poetry was the work of the Commander.

The salt industry is conspicuous along the coast of China, though a certain amount of salt is also obtained from lakes and wells inland. It is chiefly employed in the preservation of fish and vegetables. Fishing-boats are constantly in evidence as one travels from port to port. The Chinese are good seamen and have even sailed round the world in some of their native vessels, which, though rather unwieldy, are solidly constructed for hard usage.

Undoubtedly there is much of interest to be seen along the China coast and many of the maritime ports are very healthy places in which to live. Weather may be rough and foggy occasionally, but the

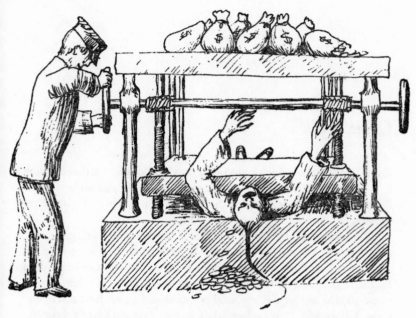

Souvenir of a dinner-party on a U.S. gunboat, found inside a pie.

Customs Service has established a number of lighthouses and meteorological stations at suitable points on the islands and rocky promontories of the coastal provinces. Yet it is advisable to remember the mnemonic rule for typhoons in the Orient:

> June, too soon;
> July, stand by!
> August, you must,
> September, remember!
> October—all over.

CHAPTER 11

China Talk

On my way out to China I studied a small colloquial textbook which had been presented to me by our London office, and on arrival at Singapore I tried speaking to the Chinese shopkeepers in their own language. They all answered 'No savee!'

I was advised by an old China hand to learn pidgin English first, as it is more or less a literal rendering of Chinese into basic English, with a small admixture of Portuguese. It is definitely not the pidgin English of the stage Chinaman. I spoke to a Chinese gentleman who came aboard at Hong Kong, and pointing to a good-sized fish in our wake I inquired, 'He belong what name?' He replied cryptically, 'Have got plenty water inside.' This being interpreted means that it was a large fish and so most of it was below the waterline! This *lingua franca* may have been useful in the old trading days, when few foreigners spoke Chinese and no Chinese knew English, but happily it is now gradually passing out of use.

One of my aunts was a missionary teacher in China, and she also gave me a textbook on the language which she had written herself, together with another of her books called *A New Thing*, describing her life in Szechuan. In the latter publication she remarks on the initial difficulty of mastering the tones of the Chinese language:

While Ch'en-ta-ko, our cook, was at Han-chong, we engaged a young man to take his place. He knew nothing about cooking for foreigners, so we had to teach him. I must tell you of an amusing mistake he made. One evening we had some beef rissoles for tea, and the man was told to add some gravy and warm up the remainder for breakfast. When they appeared on the breakfast-table, they looked brown and appetizing, and we commended our cook. But the first taste made us exclaim. 'What had he done?' Then we discovered that, instead of using gravy, he had stewed the rissoles in treacle. This is how the mistake had come about; *t'ang* is gravy, and *t'ang* is also treacle; but instead of saying *t'ang* in a high tone of voice, which means 'gravy' we had used a low tone, which means 'treacle'. It was a useful mistake, for we shall remember, in future, which is which.

I myself once declared that I had come from Shanghai on a *brick* (chuan), instead of a *steamer* (ch'uan), having omitted the slight pause, or aspiration, which should be made in the middle of the word.

On arrival at my first station I was immediately provided with a Chinese name to which I might be referred, if necessary, in Chinese office correspondence and reports. It was Wei Li-shih, meaning Imperial Upright Scholar, a name which appeared to need a lot of living up to, and was supposed to be a transliteration of my English name of Williams.

These Chinese names, generally selected by a junior clerk, are often ridiculous, as, for example, a German Assistant called Diehr, who became Ti Erh, or Number Two! When he realized that he had been forced into this secondary position he asked to be called T'ieh Kung, or Iron Duke, after a celebrated Chinese warrior of old, and his Prussian mind was highly gratified by the approval of the authorities to this alteration in his title. In my own case, when the Imperial Government was ousted by the Republican Party some years later, I asked for my own Imperial surname to be also dropped. This was allowed and I became Wen Lin-shih, or Student in the Forest of Literature. But, nevertheless, my Chinese friends continued to call me an Emperor!

I engaged my first Chinese teacher at Hankow, and, though I did not realize it, he spoke the Hankow dialect and used a good deal of the local slang. Moreover, he had an impediment in his speech. I have a good ear for sound, and the first time I was examined in the language by my Chief, the Commissioner of Customs, he told me I was giving an imitation of an old Hankow peasant, and was advised to employ a teacher with a purer accent of the Mandarin or Court dialect. I did so!

I found it very easy to speak Chinese after a few months, but the written character—aptly described as a happy painter's uncommercial shorthand—was a great stumbling block. However, I persevered for many years, in accordance with Customs Circular Instructions, and spent a great deal of money on books and teachers in my laborious attempts to become efficient.

One of my friends once expressed his desire to commence the study of Chinese, and asked me to engage a teacher for him. I accordingly arranged for my own teacher to go to him at times when I did not require him myself. A few weeks later I asked the teacher how his new pupil was shaping. He said, 'When I came the first day he learned to say "*Ming t'ien lai*" [Come tomorrow], and that is usually all he said to me on subsequent occasions! One day, however, he actually asked me to sit down and we started on the textbook you lent him. After about ten minutes he put his hand to his head wearily and seemed to be sleeping peacefully. Suddenly he woke up and bowed me out, saying, in the Shanghai dialect, "*Ossaw!*" [Hurry up!]—as if I were a rickshaw-coolie. I have never seen him since!'

During my stay at Hankow I lived in a house on the bund where there was a large Assistants' Mess, comprising members of many different nationalities. One day I said to one of them, 'Are you good at Chinese?' 'No,' he replied, 'but I can always make myself understood'. So saying he took off his shoe and threw it violently at the door, and his Chinese servant immediately came in with a whisky and soda. 'There you are,' he declared; 'it's quite easy when you know how to do it!'

A new system of examinations in the Chinese language was introduced in the Customs Service in 1911. There were to be three grades, A, B, and C. Those who could not pass C would be discharged. Those who passed C would be required to go up for B continually until they passed. Those who could not pass A would never rise to the rank of Commissioner. And those who passed A with honours, i.e. with over 80 per cent marks, would be given the preference, for promotion and appointment, above those who had not so qualified.

I decided to work for A with honours. At first I passed A except for one section—the unseen written work. The next year I passed in the final section, and received my A certificate. At the next examination I failed for the A standard, which I had already secured. I was afraid they would take away my certificate, but they did not do so. The next time I qualified for A again, and the following year I succeeded in passing A with honours.

I also obtained an honours certificate at the Chinese Language School of the Shanghai British Chamber of Commerce, and, for good measure, I took a course of Chinese at the London University when I was on my first leave after seven years' service.

Nevertheless my rate of promotion in the Service was not accelerated as promised by the Inspector-General.

At a dinner-party given by one of my colleagues, his wife remarked to me: 'My husband *never* studies Chinese. He says people who study Chinese invariably go mad!' Then, hastening to cover up her *faux pas*, she added: 'Of course, *you* are an exception to the general rule!'

William Milne, the famous Chinese scholar, wrote in 1914: 'To acquire the Chinese is the work of men with bodies of brass, lungs of iron, heads of oak, hands of steel, eyes of eagles, hearts of apostles, memories of angels, and lives of Methuselah!' I quoted this once to a junior Assistant whom I was helping in the study of Chinese, one of many, and he retorted: 'I always wondered why I could never make any progress in the language, but now I know that it's because I haven't got a wooden head and a brass body!' I suppose I rather asked for this!

One of the finest Chinese scholars in the Service was the late Sir Robert Hart. He was also one of the few Europeans who could write Chinese. There were many Commissioners in the old days who hardly knew a word of Chinese. I was once examined by one of them, who gave me a number of square pieces of paper with Chinese on one side and English on the other, and told me to memorize them. I looked at them and said, 'I think I know all these.' The Commissioner was very surprised. 'Why,' he exclaimed, 'if I knew as many characters as you do I should have been Inspector-General long ago!' This used to be a common way of learning Chinese characters, of which there are over 10,000. One man I knew had them pasted on his bedroom wall, carried a batch in his pocket, and lived in a continual atmosphere of complicated brushwork. He *did* go mad, and had to be invalided home with a special attendant to look after him. On the journey he refused to speak anything but Chinese, and declined to have a bath, because, he explained, the Chinese rarely, if ever, had baths!

Apropos of lunacy, I once had a mad Chinese teacher, although, strangely enough, he did not infect *me*. He was a Nanking man, and I read the Confucian Analects with him. He tried to persuade me to smoke opium. It would stimulate my mind, he declared, and make me a very brilliant scholar. I turned his suggestion down. Rather than become a dope-fiend I preferred to remain more or less unlettered!

My eccentric teacher had made a close study of all the great

religions of the world, which he tried one by one. He was inclined
to believe mostly in the worship of Brahma, 'for,' said he, 'all the
gods are in Brahma as cows in a cow-house!' Rather crowded, I
thought. He preferred Christianity to Lamaism, because there is only
one devil in the former, while there are several million of these
awkward customers in the latter! He told me that the worst of all
was the Baptist faith, because he was baptized by total immersion in
the winter, and caught a terrible cold! He rather liked Roman
Catholicism because the ritual was spectacular, and rather resembled
Buddhism in that respect. 'It would be good,' he remarked, 'to have
a holiday on all the saints' days, as there is one every day!' He liked
being a Seventh Day Adventist on Sunday, which is regarded by its
adherents as a weekday. The Anti-Christians once asked him to can-
vas for converts (or should I say perverts?) at twenty cents a head.
He thought this might be good business if he could persuade the
Methodists to pay twenty cents a head to get them back again into
the fold. Thus, he would have a steady income. He approached the
latter with this proposition, but unfortunately they were disinclined
to do business. As regards Confucianism, Buddhism and Taoism, he
said Taoists, to be on the safe side, often engaged Buddhist priests at
weddings and funerals, and *vice versa*, and the three religions were
but one. When I last heard of him he was in Shanghai advocating
some strange religious cult of his own invention.

I remember I was very nervous when I was first examined in
Chinese. The Examiner was hard and stern, and did nothing to make
me feel at ease. At the end of the examination I said, 'I hope I
haven't done too badly?'

He replied tersely, 'Good morning!' He failed me.

I once examined a man in Chinese who was simply palpitating
with terror. I sent to my house for a couple of stiff brandies and soda.
After that we both felt fine. He did well and I passed him with flying
colours. His promotion soon came along and his subsequent career
was exceedingly brilliant. In fact, he passed over my own head eventually. I hesitate to put the blame on the brandy! This reminds me of
a Chinese clerk whom I used to help with his English. He also rose
above me in the Service. But I soon became quite accustomed to
watching my juniors flying over me like flocks of birds. I only wished I
knew the secret!

Since then I have myself examined many persons in Chinese.
They have been of various nationalities—British, American, French,

German, Russian, Portuguese, Norwegian, Swedish, Belgian, Dutch, Japanese, and also Chinese. The reason I examined Chinese in their own language was because I was called upon to hold an examination for the Hong Kong University in 1928 of Cantonese students who had been taking a course of Mandarin, or the Court dialect. On the whole, the Germans made the best students, but the Russians came next, for they are always quick at languages. My own nationals are about the worst, with, of course, some notable exceptions.

In spite of the fact that I have studied nearly all the best modern textbooks on Chinese, I have come to the conclusion that the most practical method, after the first year's work on elementary colloquial, is to practise speaking with the natives. In order to do this I made a collection of old Chinese cash. I then ascertained the names and addresses of local Chinese gentry who collected (and there were many), and I visited them and discussed coins, which, incidentally, improved my knowledge of Chinese history. They were all glad to see me, and I made many friends and learnt to speak Chinese quite fluently by conversing with them.

I sewed the coins on cards and typed the date and description above each Imperial issue, etc., and filed them in folders on the loose-leaf system. After a time my collection grew enormously, and became too heavy to move about conveniently, especially when I was transferred to another port, so I sent it to auction in Shanghai, where it sold for about twenty-five pounds, which was a great deal more than I had paid for it.

When I arrived at my next port I found that my Chief, the Commissioner, was very fond of curios. His house was so full of them that it was hardly possible to move an inch without knocking something over. He asked me if I had any curios. 'Only one,' I replied, 'but it's a good one!'

'I should like to see it,' he said.

'I shall be delighted; here it is.' And I pointed to *my wife*!

'I used to have a collection of antique Chinese coins,' I remarked.

'I'll show you mine,' he said. To my great surprise he produced *my own* collection, which he had bought in the Shanghai auction. He declared that he had spent over twenty years collecting these coins, some of which had come from old tombs of the early dynasties, others he had secured at great expense from Chinese officials in reduced circumstances. After that, I thought it would be judicious not to claim any personal responsibility in the matter!

Regarding written Chinese, I made the mistake of buying a monu-
mental dictionary and the best translations of the classics, etc., but I
eventually discovered that there is really nothing better than the
Chinese newspaper for purposes of practical study of the document-
ary style. Textbooks soon become out of date, and the language is
changing rapidly, new terms and expressions continually being
adopted, especially from Japan.

I once served under an old Commissioner who came to the office
every day for an hour after lunch, and I always found him asleep, so
I generally took my large Chinese dictionary and dropped it at the
door to wake him up if I wanted his signature on any of the reports
and returns. So I cannot say that this dictionary has been entirely
unnecessary!

As already mentioned, the Customs Service has always encouraged
its foreign members to study Chinese. It has also published a number
of textbooks for sale to the general public. I studied Chinese assiduously and encouraged others to do so as well. I also made some textbooks for Service use. Too late I remembered the advice to a young
Assistant, quoted earlier in this book, not to learn much Chinese, and
I ask myself: 'Was my labour really necessary?' The answer echoes
the native merchant to whom I first tried to speak Chinese: 'No
savee!'

CHAPTER 12

Peking Dust

The Boxer Rising and the Siege of Peking were vividly portrayed as an exciting and colourful pageant at Olympia before I left school in England, but I remember going to see it, and very likely it was at that precise moment that China began to exercise its attraction on my youthful mind. Sir Claude MacDonald was British Minister during the siege, and it was he who nominated me for the Chinese Customs a few years later. Lady MacDonald, before she was married, was an old friend of my mother's in India. She was represented at the Olympia performance, kneeling down, wringing her hands, and begging the Legation butcher not to cut up her favourite pony for food. Very touching, of course, but quite fictional!

And now I have been to Peking myself. I have not only trodden, but also swallowed, its dust. Sometimes the air was thick with it, as it swirled in from the Gobi desert. Sometimes we also consumed a more pleasing form of 'Peking Dust', as this was the name of a common *pièce de résistance* at formal dinner-parties, being composed of a most delicious mixture of mashed chestnuts, sugar and cream, surrounded with a kind of pallisade of finger-biscuits.

I have lived longer in Peking than in any other part of China, having been stationed there twice, first as Assistant Chinese Secretary at the old Inspectorate-General of Customs for two years, when conditions were normal, as the Chinese Government still functioned there; then again for four years as Vice-President and Lecturer at the Customs College, being also in charge of the duty collection on postal parcels, and of the office and properties of the Inspectorate, which by that time had moved to Shanghai, while the Government went to Nanking.

When in the Chinese Department I not only had to set and mark innumerable Chinese examination papers covering all the Treaty Ports, but I also lectured on Customs work at the Customs College for the training of Chinese for the Service, and examined the students at the end of each term. On my second visit to Peking, *lit.*: 'Northern Capital', I found it had been renamed Peiping, 'Peace in the North', a name which it had had before in the early Ming Dynasty. It has had many names in the past, the only steady one being the literary designation, which remains Yenching, or the 'City of Swallows'.

The former Imperial glories and pageantry had given place to the more sober and practical Republic, and, when the Government also departed to Nanking, together with our Head Office and its 'Royal Family', I must say I felt very much like a disembodied spirit wandering about in the fourth dimension. The British Minister, who was still there, asked me if I was the sole representative of the Inspectorate-General, and I hardly knew how to describe my position. Possibly I was a kind of unofficial I.G.—without portfolio!

The ancient capital of China presents a beautiful appearance as viewed from its surrounding wall, where one could see an entrancing vista of temples and palaces, their curving roofs glittering with blue, green and yellow porcelain tiles, among the groves of trees with which the city abounds.

In order to see it still better I went up in an aeroplane. This was the first time I had ever been up in the air—except figuratively. My mother came to see me off. We went by car to the aerodrome, and on the way we skidded and overturned in a ditch, but managed to crawl out unhurt! Twenty Chinese coolies pulled the car on to the road again. This was a good sign. Better a crash on land than from the sky!

It was a Junkers plane, and there were several other passengers, including some Indians who were sick all the time, especially when we banked and hung edgewise. The window next to me was broken and mended with strips of sticking plaster, but I managed to see out. It was a wonderful sight!

My bird's-eye view showed me that Peking is not only one city, but a veritable conglomeration, or nest of cities, one within the other —like a Chinese puzzle. The shape of the whole collection is that of a square imposed upon a parallelogram. This square figure, in the north, consists of the Tartar or Inner City, while the adjoining parallelogram, in the south, contains the Chinese or Outer City. In the centre of the Tartar City is the Forbidden City, in turn surrounded by the Imperial City and its palaces, which are open to the public on payment of a small fee. At one time they held many valuable treasures, most of which were later removed by the Government.

Peking City and all its internal cities are each surrounded with separate battlemented walls of earth, concrete and brick.

Passing northwards, high above the Altar and Temple of Heaven, the former resembling a white china plate, and the latter seeming like a round blue saucer. The brilliant coloration of the roof-tiles of the numerous buildings, and the orange-red wall of the Forbidden City, stood out as prominent landmarks in a physical scale-map. From the sky, it was apparent that there are far more trees in the city than one would imagine. The principal variety is the age-old cypress, readily distinguished by its olive-green foliage.

A long caravan of camels, each one tied to the tail of the one in front, and laden with sacks of coal, was ambling disdainfully through the Chien Men, or main gate, as we rattled over it like a threshing-machine. One of the animals looked up and gave vent to a weird high-pitched scream of astonishment. Our plane waggled its wings in salute, though perhaps that was accidental.

To the west of the Forbidden City lie the three great lakes, which were artificially constructed in imitation of the well-known Hang-chow lake system.

Describing a wide circle from the Drum and Bell Towers we zoomed over the Lama and Confucian Temples, with their bright orange tiling, and finally returned, soaring and sliding across the outer Chinese city, to drop lightly on the landing-field from which we originally started in the south.

One of the most impressive objects in Peking is the Nine Dragon Spirit Screen, which stands on the shores of the North Lake in the grounds of the Imperial City. This screen is of brick faced with a marvellous design of glazed coloured tiles set together in the form of nine coiling and writhing dragons. They are so beautifully fashioned that they actually seem to be alive and ready to fight in protection of the Emperor against all evil spirits and marauders in the sacred precincts. There are said to be nine species of dragon, so this protective screen symbolizes all the dragons in existence.

The temples of Peking, both inside and outside the walls of the city, are many and varied. The most beautiful of all is the Temple of Heaven, which is situated in the south of the Chinese city, outside the main gate. It was erected in A.D. 1421. There are two round marble altars, on one of which stands the temple, with its roof of bright blue tiles. I once visited the Altar of Heaven in order to view it in the moonlight. To my disgust I found a party of noisy tourists dancing on this sacred edifice to the accompaniment of the worst form of 'hot rhythm' on a gramophone. A truly depressing experience for the Imperial shades!

I often visited the fine old Confucian Temple, to the west of which is the Hall of Classics, where Confucian ethics were expounded in former times, and the nearby Lama Temple, which was formerly one of the palaces of the Emperor Yung Lo.

In the spring of 1929, when the beautiful peach and apricot trees were showing a wealth of glorious blossom, I went by car to the Temple of the Azure Clouds outside the north wall, accompanied by the former Customs College Vice-President, Mr E. Albaster, and the Dean, Mr Huang Chi-pi, to pay our respects to the earthly remains of Dr Sun Yat Sen, whose memory is an inspiration to all Chinese to strive conscientiously for the good of their government. As I stood before the catafalque, I recollected the important and interesting fact that, in 1896, the British Government was instrumental in rescuing Dr Sun from the hands of his enemies in London, and he was thus enabled to live on and form the foundation of the present Republic of China. The Manchu Government had offered a reward of £100,000 for the capture of Dr Sun, who fled to England and was illegally arrested by the Chinese Legation in 1896, but was set at liberty by the British authorities. The work he did finally resulted in the Revolution of 1911, and his own appointment as first President of the new Republic.

It is not generally known that Dr Sun proposed to place the administration of the country in foreign hands for a few years, during which time he believed the civil war would be suppressed and all industrial resources developed. The foreign powers, perhaps unfortunately, declined to accept this responsibility, and civil war has continued.

His body was embalmed and lay in state at Peking for several years in the Temple of the Azure Clouds, and, soon after my visit there, it was conveyed by special train to Nanking, where it was enshrined in a glass coffin, in an elaborate mausoleum, costing about £200,000, on the slopes of Purple Mountain, near the old Ming Tombs. The funeral procession from the Temple to the railway station was about a mile long. The front of the engine was decorated with a large picture of the deceased. By the side of the road, small pavilions were erected at intervals for the coffin to be laid down occasionally, in order to rest the spirit.

A large portrait of Dr Sun, surmounted by the national flag, hung in a prominent position in every scholastic establishment throughout the country, and in all public buildings. Students, Government officials and representatives of the people had been accustomed to assemble once a week to render homage before this picture. The ceremony was accompanied by one minute's silence, three bows, and the singing of the National Anthem, which exalts the Three Principles of the People—Nationalism, Democracy, and Socialism, as defined by the Founder of the Chinese Republic.

A specialized cult had therefore grown up around his immortal memory, thus stimulating the people to a sense of patriotism, which had begun to fall away to some extent after the many political changes which had taken place from time to time.

The removal of the old capital to Nanking was also calculated to induce a nationalistic spirit. Peking recalled the subjugation of the country by Mongol and Manchu in the past. The Legation Quarter, with its armed guards, crenellated wall and steel gates, had long been a thorn in the flesh of the Chinese Government. The position of Peking was also geographically unfavourable, especially as it was not far away from the Manchurian frontier, where invasion by the Japanese might be expected at any time, and actually did occur eventually. Nanking occupied a central position. From Nanking the great Hung Wu threw off the Mongol yoke, and founded the Ming Dynasty in 1368.

By this move, the foreign Legations were left high and dry, as the tide of national life gradually receded to the south. So the Ambassadors and their suites were compelled to move themselves to Nanking as well. But life was very gay, as I remember it, in the old days. I had the honour of being presented to the late Chinese President Hsu Shih-ch'ang at Peking in 1920, on the occasion of his birthday, when he gave his framed photograph to be hung in the various Custom Houses in China. I also attended various official functions held in the Forbidden City. Diplomats and military officers came in uniform, and civilians were required to wear evening dress, although the ceremonies took place during the day-time. Military medals were very much in evidence, and I remember meeting a stalwart Chinese general at one of these levees who was bedecked with medals all across his chest and under his arms as well! No doubt he had been very successful in the suppression of rebels and bandits on many occasions.

The various Legations celebrated their national festivals most punctiliously with receptions, and also with dinners and dances at the Hotel de Pekin; the King's birthday, St George's, St Patrick's, and St Andrew's Days by the British, George Washington's birthday by the Americans, and the Taking of the Bastille by the French, etc.

I remember one St Andrew's dinner when we were waiting for the high spot of the feast, the Piping-in of the Haggis, which was late in arriving. The Master of Ceremonies reassured us by announcing: 'They have'na killed the MAN yet!'

On the anniversary of Washington's birthday, an elaborate dinner-party was given one year, which I attended as a guest of Mr L. C. Arlington, the late American sinologue. Mr George Bernard Shaw had just arrived on a visit to Peking. He was, of course, invited to join the festivities, but—like George Washington—he could not tell a lie, and declined on the grounds that he had a special diet and preferred to dine alone. Thus, it seemed he demonstrated the philosophical significance of his conception of the superman. He accepted, however, a copy of Mr Arlington's masterly book, *The Chinese Drama*, and, in return, presented a complete edition of his own dramatic productions.

I was acquainted with five British Ministers in Peking: Sir Claude MacDonald, Sir John Jordan, Sir Beilby Alston, Sir Miles Lampson (later Lord Killearn), and Sir Alexander Cadogan. Sir Miles Lampson was formerly First Secretary under Sir John Jordan. Tall and of commanding presence, he was always most hospitable, and I have memories of many delightful receptions given by him in the magnificent Chinese open pavilion opposite to his official residence. Here I mixed with a thoroughly cosmopolitan throng of diplomats and military officers in uniforms glittering with decorations, and ladies and children attired in brilliant colours. The hollyhocks and snapdragons made a beautiful show in the garden plots and along the old bullet-scarred Legation walls. The officers of the British Legation Guard also gave dinners and dances, and the Legation Chapel ministered to our spiritual needs.

The British Legation was raised to the status of an Embassy in 1935, and other Legations have followed suit. Legation Street was quite unique. It seemed to be reminiscent of some quiet road in an old cathedral town. Cool, peaceful, and free of dust, it was pleasant to enter its formal and orderly precincts after the contrasting heat and hubble-bubble of the Chinese *Hutungs*, or byways. Legation

Street was originally a canal with muddy banks, but it was filled in and made a fine thoroughfare. The Legation Quarter was administered by a diplomatic Commission from 1902 to 1945, when it was handed back to Chinese control.

It fell to my lot, when the Inspectorate was removed from Peking, to pack up a quantity of archives and most of the furniture of eighteen Staff houses, and send them to Shanghai. I consumed a full peck of dust—Peking dust—in doing this! I was then instructed to rent out the empty houses to the public. I worked out a scheme for dividing the office into four sets of apartments, or flats, the I.G.'s house also into four, and the Junior Assistants' Mess into two. This scheme was approved by the 'powers that be' and more rentals were thereby obtained.

I actually lived for a time in one of the flats in the old I.G.'s house, my drawing-room being his former study—where my Letter of Appointment was signed over thirty years previously—and I wondered if Sir Robert Hart's spirit was displeased that his old residence, built in the shape of the letter H, for Hart, had become altered out of all recognition. Walls were demolished here and there, doors bricked up, and the vast drawing-room cut into several smaller rooms. At first we called this newly adapted building 'Hart Apartments', but this name was subsequently changed to 'Haikuan (Customs) Apartments'.

The Customs is actually under the direct control of the Kuan Wu Shu, or Revenue Council, the Director of which, Mr Shen Shu-yu, I had the pleasure of meeting in 1933, when he invited me to lunch and asked me to use my influence as Vice-President of the Customs College at Peking to negotiate for the sale of that establishment, as it was intended to build a new College at Woosung, near Shanghai. The President of the College invited me to go with him to Nanking to be presented to the Chief Executive, General Chiang Kai-shek, and I always regretted that I did not take the opportunity of doing so.

Among other interesting people I met in Peking were Mr T. V. Soong, former Minister of Finance, and Admiral Tsai ting-kan, who was Director of the Revenue Council in 1917. The latter was a Yale graduate, and died in 1935 at the age of seventy-four. He was noted for the excellence of his after-dinner speeches. The Co-Director of the Revenue Council at that time was Sun Pao-ch'i, who invited me to the best Chinese dinner I ever attended, in recognition of my work at the Customs College. The menu contained poetical allusions to the dishes provided. Outstanding in my memory is the ducks' tongues soup.

I once met an American globe-trotter, who had set himself the task of dragging his weary length around the world without finding any 'sermons in stones or good in anything'. We travelled together by train from Peking to Chinglungchiao, the station for the Great Wall. He was a millionaire suffering from dyspepsia, which, he said, was due to the bad food in the hotels. He offered me some sandwiches, for which I thanked him, but, when he asked the price and the train attendant told him they were fifty cents each, he said it was like eating money and withdrew his offer! He declared the Great Wall to be 'just a lot of broken bricks', and the beautiful palaces of the Forbidden City, with their gleaming tiles of Imperial yellow, to be 'a mere collection of poached eggs'! A man like that should go far and accomplish nothing!

The Great Wall, which I visited several times, twists all over hill and dale, and is, of course, one of the seven wonders of the world. According to an ancient legend, a pure white spirit horse descended from Heaven and trotted over the country from Mongolia to the sea, thus indicating the desired position of the necessary rampart against the barbarians. The design was then plotted out in sand on a marble table by the Grand Secretary of State, under the directions of the Emperor Shih of the Chin dynasty, 246 B.C. The length of the wall, from Shanhaikuan to the western borders of Mongolia, is two thousand five hundred miles. If it were superimposed round the coast of Britain, there would still be five hundred miles to spare.

I have also visited the old Imperial Mausolea at Peking and Nanking. The approach to the Ming Tombs outside Peking is across a vast plain through a beautiful five-span marble archway some fifty feet high and seventy-five feet wide, and along an avenue of colossal stone figures of men and animals. Three arches of an old marble causeway lead to the tombs in high mounds of earth.

Dr Davidson Black, the late palaeontologist, who was connected with the excavation of the skull of *Sinanthropus Pekinensis*, or the Peking Man, and Dr A. W. Grabau, the biological expert, were residents of Peking in my time. Dr Grabau held the theory that our animal ancestors came from the region where the Himalayas arose by convulsions of nature, which drove out the anthropoid apes into China. Conditions of living there were different and necessitated certain adaptation and evolution of form, such as shortening of arms, power to walk erect, and reduction of jaw, owing to increased use of hands and weapons. The new mountain ranges gradually affected the weather, and caused the heavy dust-storms, which deposited the loess soil over the north of China. Under the loess we may therefore search for traces of the progenitors of early man. The survivors of the fittest went forward under the new conditions, and developed into the present-day *Homo sapiens*, after passing successfully through the vicissitudes of the glacial period, and undergoing continuous stages of evolution to the present day. The Peking Man has an ape-like jaw, and a man-like cranium, and is of pre-Neanderthal type, which places him in line with the anthropoid group. Thus there is a distinct liklihood that he is the 'missing link' we have been looking for so long and that the dust of Peking was the cradle of the human race!

Two other interesting characters, resident in Peking, were Owen Lattimore, the well-known British explorer of Mongolia and Turkestan, and Roy Chapman Andrews, an American who probably was more closely acquainted with Peking dust than any man alive, for he had sifted out quantities of the sand of the Gobi desert in his search for the eggs of the *dinosaur*, of which he eventually unearthed some good specimens, about a million years old, for the American Museum of Natural History, New York.

I eventually shook the dust of Peking off my feet with regret, and also with sorrow, for there I left the earthly remains of my dear mother, who passed away suddenly, in 1934, just before my last period of home leave became due.

CHAPTER 13

The Forest of Pencils

The Han Lin Yuan, or 'Assembly of the Forest of Pencils', was an Imperial Academy founded during the eighth century and continuing until the time of the Republic. There were about five hundred members representing the most brilliant scholars of the kingdom. They compiled dynastic histories, drafted and drew up decrees, Government publications, etc. The higher members were *ex officio* Councillors to the Emperor.

In each of the eighteen provincial capitals there was a Kung Yuan, or Examination Hall. Some of these covered over sixteen acres, and were a collection of about eight thousand cells surrounded by a wall. Examinations for the various degrees were held triennially and lasted nine days, during which time the candidate was not allowed to leave his cell. He supplied his own food and bedding. There might be a death, in which case the body was lifted over the wall, as the gates were not allowed to be opened during the examination.

In order to qualify for a degree it was necessary for the student to assimilate enormous quantities of classical literature and write essays and poetry on subject-matter derived therefrom. It was a colossal strain on the memory.

There were three degrees: *Hsiu-ts'ai*, Bachelor; *Chü-jen*, Master; and *Chin-shih*, Advanced Scholar. From the last were selected the Members of the Forest of Pencils, after further weeding out by competitive examination at the capital. The one who passed out at the top was known as *Chuang-yüan*, or Senior Wrangler—the first scholar in the Empire.

As any graduate was a potential official, bribes were sometimes offered to the Examiners, to be paid from the salary received when employed by the Government, but there were, of course, a large majority of honest competitors who only wished to enjoy the great respect which was accorded to the *litterati*. Some more astute

Examiners insisted on cash in advance, and this was indicated by the student with special signs on his papers.

The punishment for cribbing at the examinations was the cangue (Portuguese: *Canga*, neck-yoke), which was inflicted, not only on the offender, but also on his father and tutor as well! Moreover, he was forbidden to compete again.

The average age of the competitors was thirty, though some of them went on trying until they were over eighty!

This educational system had its drawbacks. While it produced a highly artistic man with a much-developed memory, yet there was a failure 'to select the good and discard the superfluous' in the curriculum of studies.

Education in China, as I watched it for some thirty years, has undergone considerable evolution. Formerly, it was believed that the ancient classics contained nearly everything necessary for an educated man's knowledge. The resultant graduate had his brain forcibly filled with much material which he was unable to put to any practical use, and, moreover, his health was often ruined by too much burning of the midnight oil and a total lack of healthy exercise. 'For many years', wrote a famous scholar, 'I never looked at my garden.' In the San Tzu Ching, or 'Trimetrical Classic', the first textbook for beginners, rules are laid down for classical study, and examples given of the pursuit of knowledge under exceptional difficulties. As, for example, the poor boy who tied his books to the horns of the ox and studied them assiduously while ploughing the fields; others who read by moonlight reflected from the snow, or with the aid of glow-worms, and one who tied his own hair to a beam to keep himself awake. In fact the whole theory was 'All work and no play'.

In order to assist in the reorganization of the existing state of education, the Chinese Customs Service began to take a hand by the inauguration in 1862, at Peking, of the *T'ung Wen Kuan*, a college for the training of official interpreters, as first constituted. In 1866 science was added to the subjects of instruction. In 1869 its scope was further extended and two auxiliary schools were opened in Shanghai and Canton. Customs employees were detached to lecture in these establishments.

Gradually the scholastic system of the country was improved, but at first the modern subjects introduced were far too numerous, and it became impossible for the student to assimilate more than a smattering of each. Now, however, a better sense of proportion is being shown in these matters.

In 1900, the *T'ung Wen Kuan* was merged in a missionary establishment known as the Peking University, and various technical and other schools were opened in different parts of China. In many of these schools foreign instructors were engaged.

In 1908 the Customs College was opened in Peking for the training of Chinese for the Indoor Staff of the Customs Service. Of the Co-Directors, one was Chinese, appointed by the Shui-wu Ch'u, or Revenue Council, and the other was a foreign member of the Customs Inspectorate. Admittance was by competitive examination, and the teaching given by a staff of Chinese and foreign professors, some of the latter being drafted from the Customs.

When I was appointed Vice-President and Lecturer at the Customs College in 1929, I had already had a year's experience of lecturing there, ten years before, on Customs Regulations and International Treaties, but I now found that there were many more students, and the classes were correspondingly larger. The curriculum had also been very greatly extended and comprised the following subjects:

1 History of the Chinese Customs Service.
2 Customs Regulations and Procedure.
3 Customs Statistics.
4 Customs Preventive Work.
5 Customs Examination and Appraising.
6 Commercial Geography.
7 International Treaties.
8 Business Organization and Management.
9 Indexing, Précis, and Correspondence.
10 Chinese Literature.
11 Chinese Dispatch Writing.
12 English.
13 French.
14 Russian.
15 International Trade.
16 International Law.
17 Commercial Law.
18 History of Economic Thought.
19 Foreign Exchange.
20 Advanced Accounting.

21 Insurance.
22 Problems of Public Finance.
23 Chemistry.
24 Transportation.
25 Elementary Accounting.
26 Elementary Statistics.

I lectured at various times on the first nine of these subjects, and latterly a Customs Appraiser was detached, at my suggestion, to revise the specimens of imports and exports in the College Sample Room, and to give technical instruction in piece goods, etc.

I was appointed I.G.'s Representative on the Examining Committee for Customs Travelling Scholarships in 1930 and 1931. The object of these scholarships was to enable students of the College, with Customs experience, to study Customs Administration in foreign countries. I set and marked some of the examination papers in this connection, and others were set by other lecturers on the College Staff.

I very soon came to the conclusion that education is the pursuit of information, the collection of fragments of experience, either of oneself or of others, and the fitting of them all together in proper sequence. I found that, in educating others, I had first to prepare the material for my lectures very thoroughly beforehand. After several years of this intensive process I certainly knew a great deal more myself!

Under the new Republic, educational reform was taken in hand, and the curriculum of studies was revised; modern science was required, and less attention was paid to the more abstruse parts of the archaic literature. However, centuries of memorization of poetic phraseology had created a mind capable of prodigious efforts, and the student, as before, was still expected to absorb knowledge like a sponge. The new studies, nevertheless, were more difficult in many ways, hence they were often only half assimilated and the youthful brain became much confused.

At this juncture came a Communistic influence, which swept like a wave over the country, and had its own effect on the schools. Every student considered himself a potential saviour of his country. Associations were formed which frequently took an active part in politics. After a time, the Government began to control the activities of the students, who resented this interference because the scholar had always been placed on a pedestal in the past and was treated with supernormal respect. As a net result, there was a certain lack of discipline in many scholastic establishments. Nowadays, however, a more practical system of education is gradually being developed, and we may certainly expect to see a very highly cultured race in the not too distant future, from which important results are likely.

Peking contained, in my time, about thirty establishments of professional or college rank, with 14,000 students—one-third of all those in China—and 11,000 students of middle school standing. It was certainly a seat of learning.

I have closer and more lengthy connection with the Customs College than almost anybody else in the Service. I put in about six years' lecturing there, and set and marked several thousand examination papers. A synopsis of each lecture was printed by the Customs College Press and distributed to each student. I worked out a special series of lectures from Customs records and my own experience and notes, on the general work of all ranks of the Service from the lowest to the highest. I also had various textbooks on Customs Indoor and Outdoor work printed for the use of the students, and, at my recommendation, the College was supplied with Customs publications for its library.

I sometimes had to set papers for Chinese with middle school or college diplomas for the entrance examinations, and finally for those who graduated out of the College, after the four years' course, into the Customs Service as Assistants or clerks.

Two branches of the College were opened at Shanghai, one being known as Customs College Branch No. 1 (Marine), and the other as Branch No. 2 (Outdoor). I visited these two branches in 1933, the former being situated at 200, Route Prosper Paris, and devoted to the preparation of Marine Officers for the Customs Revenue Cruisers, and the latter, at 222, Connaught Road, for training young men for work as Tidewaiters in the Outdoor Staff.

Apart from my lectures at the Customs College, I was also called upon to lecture at another educational establishment on Business Organization and Commercial Products. The Inspector-General had no objection to my doing so, and the Customs College samples came in handy for illustrating my work. The students here were inclined to learn everything off by heart for examination purposes. One day a student rose and asked if I would kindly lecture in a general way on commercial products, without giving any of the names of the products, as they found it very difficult to learn the names! But, of course, a study of commercial products without their names would be tantamount to a study of anatomy without bones, geography without places, or history without dates. I displayed samples of most of the products and described their fundamental origins and usage. Naturally this required reference to their botanical or chemical nature, process of manufacture, and employment in the various industries. Perhaps the particular student found the effort of intelligent concentration a little too strenuous for him.

This College, to my surprise, was co-educational—a very new departure in China—and I had several girl students in my classes. These maidens had long hair, which they used very skilfully as a curtain behind which they were able to arrange their private notes, and thus copy out the necessary answers to the questions set in the examinations! I felt a little embarrassed at first when I drew aside their raven tresses in order to confiscate the 'cribs'! The boys mostly employed their voluminous sleeves, as well as the old English method of placing the copy under the desk, and using the knee to bring it forward into view as required. They considered the teacher was quite justified in catching them cribbing and taking the crib away, but to reduce the marking on the cribbed material was regarded as extremely unfair.

Towards the China New Year holidays they became a little boisterous, and one winter's day I came into the classroom and found a snow-man had been erected in the corner. As the floor was of stone, I made no comment, but the heat of the stove gradually melted the snow-man, much to the general amusement. At the same time, however, a large mass of snow fell from the ceiling on my head! Evidently snowballs had been thrown up to the ceiling for the special purpose of giving me a shower-bath. The ragging of masters, apparently, is not the monopoly of British schools.

In spite of these occasional outbursts of high spirits, I got on very well with the students, and I was sorry when the time came for me to leave them.

I found that one of the most successful methods of enforcing discipline in Chinese Colleges is the system of discredits, or black marks, for each offence, three black marks entailing expulsion. This hits at the Chinese horror of loss of face or dignity. In one case, an insubordinate student even tried to drown himself in the swimming-pool when he was threatened with a black mark, so he was given another discredit for attempting suicide, whereupon he proceeded to break up all the rice-bowls in the kitchen, which rather disorganized the culinary arrangements. By this time, however, he considered he had saved his face by protesting in this spectacular manner, so he bought a new set of rice-bowls and was careful not to acquire the third and fatal black marking!

On the whole, I found the work most interesting and congenial, and I trust I have done something towards the suitable preparation of the budding youth of China for their struggle in the battle of life; and that what information I have been able to instil may, perhaps, prove to be of some practical use—even including the *names* (often quite useful) of the various commercial products of the world in which they live.

But, after all, as Emerson points out, 'The chief product of a community is not its exports, its manufactured goods, or its wealth, but rather the kind of people it turns out.' I did my utmost to turn out a good type of recruit for the Chinese Government service.

'The main imports of China', rather surprisingly wrote a Chinese student in an examination paper, 'are opium, gunpowder and moving pictures!'

I suppose it *is* really difficult to remember names. For instance, another pupil enumerated the different parts of a steamer as:

Crane-buoy

Hanker

Room for Steering-man

Guest-chambers

Dinner-place

Four Bells

It is, of course, important for a Customs officer to know his way about a ship, but smuggling in a 'crane-buoy' would be rather difficult to detect!

To the question 'Name six of the largest rivers in the world' the ingenious answer was given: 'The Yangtze, the Columbia, and the others are of no importance!'

India was strangely described as 'a country in the *Philippines* belonging to *Japan* and situated in *America*'! Of course, it nearly belonged to Japan once, and it is difficult to say to whom it belongs now! It has been aptly called a nation of many nations.

There is some truth in this essay on London:

'London is situated on the south bank of England. Its climate is moderate but a little wetty. It is sometimes warm and sometimes cold, but is always spread over by a dense fog, which makes the people blind and short-sighted. The fine days are always harmed by the vapour of the air. The city is located on the River Thomas, which is a tributary of the River Danube. The people of London often speak to each other, "What a naughty weather is today"! '

The Thames was connected, quite conceivably, to the Danube in early ages, when England was part of the continent of Europe. And our policy is perhaps, influenced by the prevailing fog. And, moreover, if an Englishman attempted to write a description of Peking in the Chinese language, it would, very likely, not be much more accurate.

Our methods of teaching appear to interest the Chinese educational administrators, who have visited England in order to study all branches of education under the auspices of the British Council.

On my departure, the Customs College presented me with a large and beautiful silver goblet, inscribed with all the names of the Staff, together with the engraved device *Yung Chiu Wei Hao*, meaning 'For Ever Appreciated'. The students gave me a farewell dinner and concert, at which they sang in good English the old ballad, 'God be with you till we meet again'.

The Customs College was eventually closed in the summer of 1935, and it was the intention to combine it with the other two Colleges in one joint institution at Woosung, near Shanghai.

Before I left Peking I went for a last walk round the city along the top of the old Tartar wall. The green and golden roof-tiles and purple-tinted battlements were agleam in the rays of the setting sun, as were also the ruins of the old Examination Hall, with its rows of broken-down cells, like a disordered bee-hive, where the Chinese scholars of former generations competed in great discomfort for literary degrees and entry into the 'Forest of Pencils'.

Truly the sun had set on the old educational system, and now the more fortunate youth of the modern Republic has every prospect of a bright tomorrow. The New China is gradually emerging from the wreckage of the old.

CHAPTER 14

Holiday Interlude

Anaxagoras, the Greek philosopher, who is said to have been the first exponent of the atomic theory, was on his death-bed in 428 B.C. When asked what honour should be conferred upon him, he replied, 'Give the boys a holiday!'

The atomic theory has now been proved and has given us all a temporary holiday from the ravages of war. A few more atom bombs and the holiday will be permanent!

I like to think that perhaps I am a bit of a philosopher myself—probably a mixture of the epicurean, cynical, and peripatetic varieties. And, like Anaxagoras, I *do* appreciate a holiday—even on the edge of a volcano—and I have followed his good example and given a holiday to all the boys and girls of China.

By this I do not only suggest that I have relieved them of the tedium of my presence in their country. But it actually happened like this. The Emperor's birthday used to be a public holiday. When there were no more Emperors the President's birthday was substituted. But sometimes there was no President either, so, when I was serving in the Chinese Department of the Head Office, I suggested to the Inspector-General that as Governments change but the memory of Confucius lives for ever, his birthday would be eminently suitable for a permanent holiday. He agreed and instructed me to draft a letter to the Chinese Government making the proposal, which was granted. This is my tribute to the famous Chinese philosopher.

Once a year, I was myself entitled to a holiday of twenty-eight days, and I usually spent it in houseboats, junks, and launches in the lakes, rivers, and canals of China, or in travel to the neighbouring hills in the summer, and in rough shooting in the winter.

Many of my pleasure trips were made along the fertile valley of the Yangtze, that great river which rises in the mountains of Thibet and runs 3,200 miles into the Yellow Sea.

Legend has it that originally great mountains barred the passage of the stream, and the Emperor Yen employed the wizard Wu Tzu to blow on the cliffs and make a way for the waters to pass through. Hence the formation of the noted Yangtze Gorges, in the upper reaches, where the river is narrowed to a third of its usual width and the water is four hundred feet deep in some places. Limestone cliffs rise two thousand feet or more in height, while between are innumerable rapids, which are very dangerous to navigate.

During the summer of 1904 I paid a visit to Kuling on the mountains near Kiukiang. It is a most pleasant spot to escape to in hot weather. Starting from Hankow, where the temperature was one hundred and five degrees, I travelled by paddle-steamer to Kiukiang, where, taking two basket chairs slung on poles, one for my 'boy' and one for myself, and engaging some coolies to carry my trunk, I proceeded up the hills, borne by four stalwart bearers on a narrow and dangerous path. Sometimes we mounted long flights of stone stairs, where a single false step would have precipitated us headlong into a yawning chasm bristling with jagged rocks!

We made several halts *en route* for refreshments at wayside stalls; in fact, the coolies stopped whenever they came to one, and I paid for their tea and rice, of which they consumed incredible quantities. For them this was certainly 'money for jam'. After a time I decided that their digestions would not stand any more strain, so we did not stop again until we reached the half-way house. As we went along I saw a tiger standing at the entrance of a mountain cave on the other side of the valley. As I had no wish to supply *him* with food as well, we pressed on without delay!

An elderly lady missionary hove into sight on her way to convert the heathen in the regions below. I was bumped down with unnecessary violence, and so was she. It seemed I was required to change chairs with her, as hers was a Kuling chair. The coolies took this opportunity to ask for three or four times their proper fare and some haggling over prices became necessary in order to avoid walking up the mountain on foot.

Finally, after a journey of about eight hours, crossing a bridge over a waterfall, we arrived at our destination at about four p.m. A dense fog slowly descended upon us. Passing through a small street, in which there were a few Chinese houses and shops, we stopped at the Customs

Deputy Commissioner's bungalow, to which I had been invited, a spacious building with an open veranda, situated in a commanding position overlooking the settlement.

I had a pleasant holiday in this health resort, strolling about the rocks, exploring the caves, and bathing in limpid mountain pools with cascades falling in sparkling showers from above. In the afternoons I played tennis with people from Shanghai and the outports, and, sometimes, during the game, a thick cloud would suddenly appear and keep us shrouded in mist for three or four minutes, when it was impossible to see one's opponent on the other side of the net until the clouds rolled by again.

After dinner, I would take my coffee and cigar on the veranda of the bungalow, and, on a clear night, would watch the sun, a blood-red ball dipping slowly behind the hills, while in the foreground lay the little church, the post-office, the rippling stream, and the cliffside dwellings, all tinted with the rose-coloured gleams of departing day.

I had looked forward for some time to a visit to Japan, and finally, in July 1906, I left Shanghai on S.S. *Manchuria* bound for Nagasaki, with the pleasant prospect of a whole month's holiday in the Land of the Tatami (straw mat). The *Manchuria* was a well-found Pacific Mail Boat, and we had a fine passage and luxurious food.

On arrival at Nagasaki, late at night, I was requested to hand over my keys, and my luggage was taken ashore for examination. I was then solemnly interviewed by the Sanitary Authorities, who asked for a list of all the diseases I had. When I landed I found that the examination of my baggage had been carried out so thoroughly that a bottle of cod-liver oil had been broken, with disastrous results to my clothes, and the film had been removed from my camera. Being in the Customs myself, I had to appreciate this careful work on the part of the Japanese fiscal staff.

From Nagasaki I took the train to Issahayo, a journey of about an hour. From there I continued by rickshaw to Obama, a small sea-side place, at which I decided to remain. I was in my rickshaw for about four and a half hours, and passed through some very picturesque and well-wooded country on the way.

The little houses of Obama are snugly perched on the hillsides and along the shore of the circular bay, which was studded with sailing-craft of all kinds. The Ikkakura Hotel stood in a central position, so there I took up my temporary abode. My room looked out upon the bright green hills to the north, the shimmering blue sea to the west, while the main street ran along under my balcony. I used to sit and watch the kaleidoscope of passers-by—water-coolies, itinerant musicians, beasts of burden, pedlars, and *mousmés* with high-piled hair in gay-coloured kimonos.

In the early morning and evening I jumped off the veranda into the sea. A swim in the full moon in the shadow of the mountains, with the water glowing with phosphorescence, is an experience too wonderful for words.

I had brought with me a pocket handbook of the Japanese language, and in a few days I knew enough of the vernacular to make myself understood in a simple way. The first word one heard on a visit to Japan in those days was 'O-hyo', the usual form of salutation by a native to a foreigner—a new arrival receiving quite a chorus of 'O-hyos', for, as a general rule the Japanese appear to be a courteous and cheerful people. They are very artistic, too, and pay great attention to the harmonious blending of colours. The art of arranging flowers is taught in their schools. Though their houses are plain but serviceable, their dress, especially that of the women, is gay and tasteful. I wonder, now, how such a cultured people should have so far lost their sense of proportion as to attempt the conquest of the world!

There is a small abrasion of the earth's surface at Obama, and the salt water runs in and boils as a result of coming into contact with some hot matter underground; and, having boiled, is ejected from the ground, spouting sometimes to the height of eight or nine feet, the water being used for bathing purposes, and said to possess medicinal virtues.

Some people took the mud-pack treatment on the beach, where they reposed indiscriminately, covered with medicinal mud from head to foot. Every now and again an attendant went round sprinkling them with a large watering-can, for all the world as if they were so many cabbages!

As I said before, the Japanese are a very polite people. They actually draw in their breath to avoid breathing on you. They hiss alarmingly—like a snake—when doing so! This may be because they are very fond of eating raw fish. But they actually apologize to the fish for catching and eating them! There is a religious ceremony held in Japan for the propitiation of the souls of the poor fish. It is of great antiquity, and has recently been revived after falling into abeyance for about a hundred years. The service is held in a temple by fifty priests, who then assemble in a vessel in the harbour and continue their ritual of atonement for the fishes sacrificed to cruel human appetites; they are accompanied by religious music relayed from the temple by loud-speakers, and the worshippers include numbers of children in fancy dress.

It occurs to me that eating fish first and begging pardon afterwards is rather weak consolation for the piscine spirits. But the killing of living things, including fish, is contrary to the tenets of Buddhism, and the service of propitiation is a sort of laying out money in the purchase of repentance. If it is a sin to catch fish, however, I have been singularly virtuous myself—but rather against my will!

Some of the Japanese customs are very charming. They have no false modesty, and I often used to see a lady having a bath outside her front door, which is, nowadays, perhaps rather unusual, though the habit of mixed bathing, *in puris naturalibus*, is still fashionable, and a great saving in bathing-costumes!

At the time of my visit to Japan the usual style of dress for men appeared to be a black kimono, with a bowler hat and sandals, while the women wore more elaborate coloured kimonos, with a silk 'obi', or bustle, at the back, padded hair, and wooden clogs, or 'geta'. Nobody seemed to have any pockets, but, nevertheless, I was once accosted by a gentleman, sitting cross-legged on the seat of a tram-car, who said to me, in a low, mysterious voice: 'I am detectivo!' A little later he whispered hoarsely: 'Beware of the *pickpocketto*!' In these circumstances I kept a special guard over my thirteen pockets. 'Tomorrow,' he continued, 'I will meet you in the Park. We will converse together, and my English will gradually improve.' As my holiday was drawing to a close, I was unable to avail myself of his kind invitation.

From time to time I have also enjoyed periods of long leave, and have therefore made a number of journeys between England and China.

I have been to China and back again by the Trans-Siberian route. When I passed through Moscow for the second time, in July 1934, I found great changes since my last visit before the Revolution. Motor cars had taken the place of troikas, and the old cobbled streets were being excavated for the construction of an underground railway; Tall buildings, chiefly composed of a mixture of sawdust and cement, were rising up everywhere.

I and a fellow traveller entered the 'Park of Culture and Rest', where there were flowers, lawns, a lake, theatre, cinema, gymnasium, children's playhouse, etc., free to the poor, and open to others at prices graduated according to their salaries, which are all regulated by the Government.

Though the American dollar really stood at eight roubles, we were only allowed the rate of one rouble three kopecks for the American money we carried. For some reason they preferred American currency, which they called 'Valuta', and charged us G$12 for the car we hired, though we had to beat them down from G$25.

The dress of the people was very shabby, but we were informed that this matter would be taken in hand in the next six-year Plan.

From the train, it was evident that new towns were being built, mostly of wood, in all parts of the country. We passed several gangs of convicts entrained for Siberia, men, women and children, all together. I gathered they were to be employed in building work.

I bought a food ticket for use on the train, but at the stations *en route* the dining-saloon was invaded by poor peasants, who bought the food we had paid for. Consequently after a day or two it mostly ran out, and we had to depend chiefly on such supplies as we had brought with us. Travelling is said to be broadening—but this journey across the barren steppes had the effect of making us rather thin!

The Russian stations in the neighbourhood of Manchukuo were strongly fortified with sandbags and barbed wire, and there was much movement of troop-trains as we passed through.

I met a jovial Irishman on the train, who told me he had been in China, and was once travelling by rail from Shanghai to Nanking in company with a Chinese friend. When they reached the station of Soochow, the Chinese remarked, 'I always feel unhappy when I come to this place!'

'Why?'

'Because I was in this train one day with a friend, who was suddenly taken ill with heart-failure and died here!'

'How very sad for you!' said the Irishman sympathetically.

'Yes, it *was* very sad for me,' said the Chinese. 'He owed me fifty dollars!'

Berlin was under martial law when I arrived there on the third of July 1934, just after the crushing of the Anti-Nazi plot, followed by seventy-seven executions. I never dreamed of the terrible holocaust which was to follow that beginning of ruthlessness.

I arrived safely in England, after an excellent crossing from Hook of Holland to Harwich, on the following day, having taken exactly thirteen days to travel from Tientsin.

The journey by sea from England to China takes over a month. These ocean voyages became slightly wearisome on repetition, and I became very familiar with all the ports of call. I often concentrated on a study of my fellow travellers, and, following Dr Johnson's good example:

> 'Let observation with extensive view
> Survey mankind from China to Peru.'

Some passengers feel they have a mission to elevate the lives of others. I was button-holed once in the bow of the ship by an elderly gentleman. 'Are you saved?' he demanded.

'No,' I replied nervously, 'my only escape is to jump overboard!' There was also a lady with a grim, determined face who used to deposit tracts in cabin portholes, on deck-chairs, and under the plates in the dining-saloon. One of these pamphlets read: 'Where are you going to?—HELL! HELL! HELL!' This was given to *me*, and I passed it on to the next cabin, in order to carry on the good work. The venerable old clergyman who received it must have been rather taken aback! He returned it to the good lady with the remark that he was going to Bombay, and that he hoped the climate would not be so bad as was suggested by the tract!

'Do you realize,' said another of these little circulars, 'that you are burning up the children's clothes?' This was actually an indictment against smoking, but it reached the Chief Engineer, a dour and sarcastic Scotsman, who informed the lady who was responsible for bringing forward this accusation that he would have her know that he burned nothing but 'the verra best Cardiff coal' in his engines, and that if he had any children it must have been an oversight in his youth, as he had always been too careful to burden himself with a wife!

Travelling home on holiday, I once had, as my cabin mates, a youth of fourteen, whose mother had placed him in my charge, and a gentleman who came aboard late at night just before the ship sailed. The latter passenger arrived, in fact, rather suddenly, by falling down the companion-way into the main saloon, cutting his head rather badly on the bottom step, which was faced with brass. He then proceeded rather shakily to our cabin, where he immediately fell asleep in the wrong bunk (not mine fortunately). He slept the greater part of the next day, and then apologized, explaining that he had been saying good-bye to some friends and had consequently imbibed rather too freely.

He had with him a suitcase containing two handkerchiefs, a pair of socks, and a number of bottles of whisky. This was all his luggage. He never changed his clothes nor had a bath. He drank whisky all night and slept all day. He also smoked at night, and he casually threw the half-burnt cigarette-ends on the carpet, so that we had to be always on the look-out in case of fire. Sometimes he broke a bottle or a glass, on which we occasionally cut our feet. I gave him a copy of the tract on burning the children's clothes, but I was unable to pluck him, a brand, from the burning!

He used to relate long histories about how he was an Uppingham boy, and was engaged by the British Government during the war to shoot German spies in the back, etc. etc. I rather fancy he was actually a 'remittance man' returning home like the prodigal son, but he was really well supplied with money so that he could bribe the stewards to bring him plenty of drink, as he was not allowed to be served from the bar.

The Captain tried to put him ashore, but none of the port authorities would allow him to land. Eventually, he insulted some French military officers, who had to be put at his table because there was no more room, by telling them that the French were totally unprepared for the war, and had not even enough boots for the soldiers, and if they *had* proper boots they would have run away! From then on, his meals were served in his cabin, and I and the young fellow camped on deck at night. He never grumbled and was always happy. He made no objection when my young son invented a new game consisting of ejecting pellets of chewed paper through a straw, and decorating him all over with patterns, by means of this weapon, through the cabin window as he lay recuperating from his continual drinking bouts!

I have also encountered the type of boozer who gets well and truly bottled every six months or so. There was one of this kind on a French mail-boat from Marseilles. One day at dinner this individual surprised us by getting up from the table and kissing all the ladies one by one, after which he was led away by the Captain's orders, and spent the rest of the evening happily drilling imaginary troops all over the deck! It has been aptly said that 'the wine-cup drowns more than the ocean'. He told us many stories of tiger and elephant shooting, which were most interesting, though possibly rather exaggerated. I expect, if he thought he saw three animals, he fired at the middle one, and it disappeared.

I was sitting with a Chinese passenger in the smoking-room one day, when there was a scratching and scraping on deck outside. 'What is that noise?' he asked.

'Only the holystone,' I replied.

'Is that so,' he said, 'there are many sacred stones in China, covered with antique hieroglyphics, and I should very much appreciate the honour of being allowed to see the "holy stone" which is evidently being worshipped on board this ship!'

A Japanese Consul and his wife were returning home from abroad by steamer. They had a fat and smiling baby. 'You have a fine child,' my wife remarked as she passed by on deck.

'Yes,' replied the proud father, 'I got it in Paris!'

We had a passenger once for Port Said, a young and charming English girl with a rose-petal complexion, who wept bitterly when she said good-bye to her numerous admirers on board, for she was going to marry an Egyptian half-caste whom she had met in a Yorkshire village. She will probably be a social misfit, her complexion will fade, and she will often long for the sight of her native moors so far away! Another girl was going out to India to marry her fiancé, but she changed her mind and got off at Colombo with another boy-friend whom she met on board, and entrusted him with her hand and heart instead. This is quite a common occurrence!

The great Ferdinand de Lesseps stands guard at the end of the breakwater which marks the approach to the Suez Canal. I believe he has been knocked about a bit by unruly natives chafing under foreign control. But it is to be noted that the statue is, or was, *outside* the town. It is a good example to follow. I ventured into Suez with a fellow traveller on my first excursion to the East, and we had to fight our way out of it in order to avoid being forcibly relieved of all our surplus cash, which was demanded as 'baksheesh' by numerous self-appointed guides, while purveyors of unseemly postcards, and peripatetic dealers in Brummagen ware of all kinds, clamoured unceasingly for our custom. 'You give me two half-crowns I show you some pretty ladies' 'Gullee-gullee, I get a chicken out of your neck, Mr McPherson.' 'Only two pounds, my dear gentlemen, for the basket made by the wild gipsies in the desert!' These are some of the common solicitations of the villainous touts and bum-boat men of this sink of iniquity!

The burning question arises: 'Why is the Red Sea red?' Some say because it was originally caused by volcanic fracture. Others because of the reddish-brown seaweed which collects there. The Israelites crossed it near the town of Suez, where it is only a mile wide and naturally shallow, due to the sand bars. Napoleon says he crossed it, too, on dry foot (*vide* his *Mémorial de St. Hélène*, vol. I, p. 2). We shall all be able to walk over the Red Sea soon, as it is gradually silting up. Incidentally I wonder why the White Sea has not turned red! The Black Sea is so called because of the dark mud of its shores, due to the hydrogen sulphide produced by bacteria. There are no White Russians there now. They say you cannot drown in the Dead Sea, but I should be inclined to take this statement with a grain of salt.

On the ground floor of a hotel in Aden you may pay to see an exhibition containing a 'mermaid' and a 'merman'. They lie in long, coffin-like boxes, strange, dried monsters over six feet long, with leathery black skins. They have more or less human bodies, with flippers and tails, and are far from beautiful. Actually they are manatees, or herbiverous sea-cows, and they appear to have been skilfully altered by the astute Oriental proprietor in order to resemble the legendary fairies of the ocean. They are said to have been caught in the Gulf, but these creatures are usually found further south. The forepaw, or flipper, has small flat nails, and its resemblance to the human hand is supposed to have given the Manatee its name, derived from the Latin *manus*, a hand. This mammal is probably the origin of the mermaid superstition.

The French mail-boats generally call at Djibouti, a sweltering French port on the east coast of Africa, opposite Aden across the Gulf. I went ashore with a friend. There was only one tree to be seen, an artificial one made of tin, standing in front of the Governor's house, and tethered to it was a young leopard. We sat outside an alfresco inn, consuming syrup through a straw, and watching the foreign legionaries and the black and brown inhabitants. Later on we were foolish enough to enter a mosque, where we were besieged by a crew of oily ragamuffins asking for alms in the name of Allah, and we only escaped with great difficulty.

There is a long run through the Arabian Sea to Colombo. To pass away the time, we usually had deck games and a fancy dress dance. On my last voyage out to China, the Captain won the first prize for men as a very gorgeous Indian Rajah, the premier lady's costume being a Spanish marquesa with a beautiful lace mantilla made out of a window curtain. A 'prehistoric man' carried off the prize for the most original dress (chiefly conspicuous by its brevity). He was well occupied for some days after in trying to remove the dye from his body—a native decoction of brown yams which he bought at one of the ports. It had a very offensive smell, which quite spoiled my dinner. On the night of the dance the following verses appeared on the P. & O. dinner menu, which was decorated with a gay coloured design of Harlequin and Columbine:

MASQUERADE

Tomorrow comes
And all will be
As it has been before.
But for tonight
Your Troglodyte
Becomes a Troubadour.

Just for tonight
We'll lay aside
Responsibility.
I will forget my Files, and you
Your seniority.

Forget the spate
Of tasks that wait,
The letters you must write.
You shall be Columbine, and I
Your Harlequin to-night.

N.B.—TROGLODYTE—Hermit or Cave-dweller, or men that lurk in the smoking-room and do not dance.

One evening, at dinner on a Japanese mail-boat, the steward leaned over and said, in a deep and melancholy voice, to my wife, 'Excuse me, lady, your son has cut his throat!'

We rushed to the cabin and found our youngest hopeful covered with blood! He had managed to fall out of his bunk and cut his head open. He had to have it sewn up by the ship's surgeon, and was none the worse.

In the Wenchow Hills

Itinerant Barber, Hankow, 1903

Dinner-time. Cargo-coolies at Hankow, 1903

The passengers on an ocean liner gradually sort themselves out into certain distinct groups:

(1) the quiet card-players;
(2) the noisy card-players;
(3) the deck and bucket quoit experts, who take up most of the deck space;
(4) the deck-tennis exponents;
(5) the swimmers and sun-bathers;
(6) the dancers;
(7) the love-birds (generally frequenting the boat-deck);
(8) the would-be musicians, who can sing and play in any key— and always do;
(9) *me*, with book, cigar, and deck-chair, trying to read in the midst of the turmoil!

There are marvellous beach pyjamas, backless bathing-costumes, velvet slacks, coloured shorts, *et hoc genus omne*. I found that if you wear sandals it is considered *de rigueur* to apply a crimson varnish to the toe-nails; one lady even had them different colours like a collection of birds' eggs!

Always we have with us the fat, cheery, 'life and soul of the ship', who runs the ship's sweepstake on the daily number of knots covered, and the race-game with dice and human horses (the prettiest girls are always selected as horses), and who always insists on getting up the inevitable deck sports, for which he produces inappropriate prizes purchased in the barber's shop.

How interesting all this is on a first voyage. But, nevertheless, after half a dozen or so of these ocean cruises the novelty begins to wear a little thin, and now I am rather tired of what Matthew Arnold describes as 'the unplumbed, salt, estranging sea'.

I once met a number of American millionaires travelling round the world, and seeing all the sights, at an inclusive cost of one thousand pounds a head, but if anyone offered me one thousand pounds to go on a holiday round the world, I should stay at home comfortably with my cigar instead.

No, give the boys a holiday if you like, but I get more fun now in my own backyard. I have plenty of time for gardening now. My ambition has always been 'an acre of land and a cow', or, at least, a steady anchorage on *terra firma*.

CHAPTER 15

Arts and Crafts

The world is indebted to the Flowery Land for the introduction of numerous art motives, which greatly help to enrich our lives. Many of these are of great antiquity. The arts of writing and painting are, in China, very closely connected, as they are both rather similar products of the brush. The inclusion of poetry serves to round out the general harmony of an art production, such as a piece of Chinese porcelain, which may bear both pictorial and literary designs.

Many of the paints of the early artists were compounded of jade, garnet, lapis lazuli and seed pearls, ground with a pestle and mortar. The secret of composition is often lost in the mists of antiquity.

Some of the various materials, on which these designs are reproduced, also originated in China, as, for example, silk and chinaware, while art products in bronze were fabricated there as early as 2000 B.C.

As the Japanese language is based on that of China, so was their modern art a mere development from Chinese sources. The best Chinese artistic efforts, however, are still far and away superior to anything the Japanese have been able to evolve.

Paintings in the Chinese style are continually being produced long after the original has disappeared. In appraising the age and value of a painting it is, therefore, necessary to examine the nature of the material on which it is depicted.

I once engaged a Chinese artist to paint for me in water-colours, to illustrate a book on Chinese symbolism, which I afterwards published. He worked with great rapidity, and was an excellent freehand designer. Sometimes he used the long pointed nail on the index finger for shading purposes. He was also very clever at drawing Chinese characters made up entirely of birds, flowers and butterflies.

At the Peking Institute of Fine Arts, I met a man who could paint beautiful floral studies and very passable landscapes *with his tongue*! He took a mouthful of Chinese ink, rolled up his tongue lengthways, and allowed the ink to run down to the tip in a regulated flow, like a fountain pen. He then painted the picture with the tip of his tongue. 'He who is in harmony with Nature,' said Confucius, 'hits the mark without effort and apprehends the truth without thinking.' But it is rather difficult to hit the mark with your tongue!

I once visited a Chinese dentist who displayed, with great pride, a landscape picture he had made in rosewood, inlaid with extracted teeth—a silent but grim evidence of his craft! Thus were many sufferers tortured to make—not a Roman holiday, but an Oriental landscape. He stopped a tooth for me, and the stopping fell out in less than a week. As a dentist he was an excellent artist. He only charged a dollar, and it was worth it to see the picture!

The Chinese artist has good eyes, a steady hand, and unlimited patience. I have seen a small disc of ivory, about the size of a shilling, on which were engraved some two hundred and fifty characters. In Hankow, I remember watching a man carving an elaborate design, embodying men, animals, trees, and flowers, on the restricted surface of an ordinary peach-stone; in order to see well enough he was using a drop of water in a cleft stick to magnify his work, which took him three weeks to accomplish! I have also seen portraits cut in relief on a grain of rice.

The importation of curios over a hundred years old is free of duty in America. Many an unwary tourist returning to the States laden with 'genuine' antiques from the Orient discovers, to his regret, that he has been deceived by the astute curio-dealer, and has to pay duty after all.

The term 'curio' is a much-abused one, and, strictly speaking, should only apply to the unimpeachable antique; there are numerous adaptations of Chinese articles specially concocted for foreign consumption—examples of spurious Orientalism or chinoiserie—which are loosely described as curios when retailed to the unsuspecting tourist. It is fairly safe to say that very few genuine pieces of great value are to be found, except in the hands of collectors, for China has been all but combed clean of authentic articles, and imitations are all the more plentiful in consequence.

I was offered a bronze bowl in Tientsin some years ago for five thousand dollars (then five hundred pounds). It was a magic bowl of the Chou dynasty, 1122 B.C., decorated with two dragons and the symbols of thunder and clouds. The 'magic', which added to its value, consisted in filling it with water, and running the finger round the edge, when it produced a noise like the howling of the wind, and, at the same time, the vibration caused the water to rise up in the form of a sacred mountain in the centre. It was undoubtedly an object of veneration and used in the archaic nature worship which is the basic religion of the Chinese. The same 'magic', however, can also be obtained from an ordinary fingerbowl!

Old Chinese roof-tiles are an interesting study. They are often of glazed earthenware in monochrome colours such as yellow, green, blue, purple, etc., and carved into dragons, birds, animals, and human figures. The old buildings have sets of such tiles set along the centre and corners of the roof. The number depended upon the rank of the occupier of the premises. In Peking there is frequently a ridge tile in the shape of a man riding a hen at the outer corner of the roof. This figure represents the tyrant Prince Min of Ch'i State, 283 B.C., who, after being defeated by certain other States, was strung up to the projecting roof and left there until he died. The reason why his effigy is riding a hen is that, with the weight of the Prince, the bird cannot fly down, and the back avenue of escape over the roof is guarded by a dragon, phoenix, lion, unicorn, magic horse, and one of the sons of the dragon, known as the *Ch'ih-wen*, usually placed on roofs to guard against fire. There should always be an odd number of such figured tiles, as the odd numbers come under the influence of *Yang*, the principle of light and life. Thus it is evident that a wealth of antique symbolism may be found by merely looking at the roof of a Chinese house!

I was once admiring a set of these interesting tiles on a palace in the Forbidden City when a Chinese accosted me furtively, saying, 'If you will select any of these tiles you like, I will take them off for you at night and sell them to you!' I could not bring myself to accept this vandalistic offer, but, judging from certain *lacunae* or blank spaces on the roof, it was quite clear that others had not been so squeamish. I must confess that one day, when I was visiting the Altar of the Sun, I removed a beautiful dragon tile from the top of the surrounding wall. However, my conscience gave me no rest, and, some days later, I went back and returned it to its place!

Chinese idols are of clay, wood, brass, or gilded bronze. They are often skilfully made, and many are of great age. They are generally hollow, and a heart or internal organs of gold may occasionally be found inside. In one presented to me I discovered a piece of apple-green jade, a small carved ivory jar, three crystal beads, and a folded sheet of red paper on which was written in black ink: 'The Sacred Five Viscera of the God.' The five viscera, namely the heart, liver, stomach, lungs, and kidneys, symbolize the emotional feelings.

The best carving of ivory and jade is done at Canton and Peking. For some years I possessed a piece of fossil wood, which I had carved into an ash-tray at Peking. The carver told me he had never carved anything so hard, and that it was much harder than jade. Ningpo and Shanghai are noted for the excellence of their fine furniture and wood carving. The old red-wood carvings are very interesting, and I have a collection of figures which show different expressions on their faces. There are also good Chinese red-wood carvers at Singapore, where material for working is easily obtainable.

Looking back to the old days, I always regret the passing out of fashion of that most beautiful and artistic device of the Dragon, which was the symbol of the Imperial dignity in China, until the formation of the Republic. The Forbidden City of Peking, where the Emperor and Empress resided, surrounded by the officers of their court, is full of conventional representations of this divine and benevolent monster. He appears carved in stone pillars and steps in the courtyards. He coils gracefully along the ridges of the roofs. He looks down from the ceiling of the audience-chamber. He stands guard in heavy bronze at the gates. He gazes out from doors, screens, carpets, walls, even from the back and front of the Imperial robes, and from the gilded throne itself. Many of the priceless treasures of the Palace bore the bold and majestic design of the Dragon. The emblem of the Empress was the Chinese Phoenix, that gay-plumaged bird of good omen.

When the Emperor carried out his annual worship of the Universe at the Temple of Heaven in Peking, standing on the central stone of the large round marble altar in the open air, he made obeisance to the Supreme Being, gloriously apparelled in his gorgeous Dragon robes. He was alone before Heaven—his only superior. A truly magnificent conception!

Until the Revolution of 1911, the elaborate silk-embroidered costumes of the Chinese were good examples of the elegance of Chinese artistry. Those worn on ceremonial occasions were particularly elaborate and beautiful. Males were more gaily dressed than females, but the reverse is now the order of the day. Nothing was

more impressive than the old Chinese long gown, richly and colour-
fully decorated, and accompanied by the cue, or tail, of plaited black
hair drooping gracefully down the back. The sleeve was shaped like
a horse's hoof, while the cue was reminiscent of the waving tails of
the chargers ridden by the invading Manchus, who wore it as a
graceful tribute to the animal to which they owed so much.

The cue was discarded after the Revolution, when there was a
drastic change in dress. There was an attempt to give up the use of
the long robe in favour of a short coat, and a new form of official
dress was laid down by Presidential Mandate in the Government
Gazette. It was to consist of 'a tall hat and a long black coat'—no
mention at all being made of nether garments. At first the new instructions created considerable confusion of mind. I happened to be
stationed at a small treaty port at the time, and my advice was asked
by the local Chinese officials as to trousers. I advised them to have
them made by a Shanghai tailor, together with the rest of the suit.
However, it was apparently considered that the new outfit could be
produced more economically by the local tailors, but the top-hat
presented greater difficulty. Eventually the tailor and the carpenter
combined forces to manufacture the necessary headgear, which was
constructed on a framework of bamboo rings reinforced with wire
and covered with black satin. The resulting article bore a strong
resemblance to a pagoda!

The black coat was almost down to the heels, and, with the
pagoda hat, grey flannel trousers, brown boots, and a large and
brilliant peony in the buttonhole, a remarkable *ensemble* was completed. Although it strictly followed the Government Regulations, it
would not perhaps have been quite *de rigueur* in Mayfair!

Of course, gradually, sartorial improvement began, until, nowadays, the modern Chinese looks as well, if not better, than any
habitué of the West End of London. Foreign clothes are not actually
very popular at present on account of their cost as compared with
Chinese. It was possible, in those days, to obtain a complete set of
Chinese garments for five dollars or less than ten shillings. Foreign-
style hats and shoes are, however, much affected. The Chinese grace
Western garb better than the Japanese, or indeed any Oriental, as they
have slender and graceful figures as a general rule, while the Japanese
are chiefly bow-legged from their continual habit of squatting on
the floor.

The Dragon used to figure largely on the former Chinese Orders

of Merit. China is responsible also for the creation of the 'Single
Rhinoceros Medal', the 'Brilliant Jade with Red Cravat and Blue
and White Border', the 'Order of the Civil Tiger', and many others
with equally exotic names. One of my colleagues was awarded the
'Order of the Million Elephants and the White Parasol', but this is
an Indo-China decoration. Medals and orders galore were dished
out wholesale by the Manchu Government, and the succeeding
Government. Even I got one. It was called the 'Third Class Order
of the Excellent Crop'. A friend of mine wrote and congratulated
me on this, saying that he supposed the distinction carried with it
the right to *wear a cue*!

The arts and crafts of China owe much to the work of the Customs
Service, whose Commissioners in the various ports continually study
the trade of the country and provide all possible facilities to the
merchants. Every year they compile a Trade Report which is
published and summarized by the Customs Statistical Department
and is a great help to Chambers of Commerce and traders in general.
Until about 1904, the Commissioners also undertook the collection
of specimens and working models of arts and crafts which they
dispatched to the periodical trade exhibitions throughout the whole
world. The catalogues of these Chinese trade exhibits provide very
interesting reading.

The Statistical Department has also published many 'Yellow
Books' on separate articles of the China trade, such as silk, tea, jute,
beans, skins, etc., which are of great value to economists. In particular
may be mentioned a very scholarly production by Ernest Watson,
Tariff Expert, entitled 'The Principal Articles of Chinese Commerce'.

Thus the Chinese Customs has always encouraged and fostered
the import and export trade—the goose that lays the golden eggs of
prosperity—in the interest both of the people of China and of the
revenue of her Government.

CHAPTER 16

The Lighter Side

The bushrangers of Australia are said to have organized a system of confederates for the circulation of news of police movements. This became known as the 'bush telegraph'. The African native does it with drums. But the Chinese appear to manage it by telepathy. And they do not confine their investigations to the police, but also to anything else which may turn out to be to their interest or advantage.

Hence, there is no servant problem in China, nor is it necessary to advertise for domestic labour. No sooner does a stranger put in an appearance in any part of the country, and requires a 'boy' or a cook, than, by some mysterious method unknown to science, the fact immediately becomes known to the great standing army of unemployed, who then proceed to lay siege to the new arrival!

When I arrived at my first station in China, the first thing I did was to engage a servant. This was easy, because half a dozen Chinese males, ranging from the ages of fourteen to forty-five, were waiting in the hall of the Mess for me. I engaged the ugliest one and installed him as my boy.

He was very clever, and always anticipated my wishes. He once even went to the extent of taking my keys, opening my money-drawer, and taking out some money to pay my bills, evidently labouring under the strange delusion that he was saving me trouble, though not money. When I had a friend to stay with me for a few days, I told the boy to supply him with sheets, towels, and anything else he wanted. He gave him almost everything I had, including my sponge, tooth-brush, fountain-pen, and patent-leather boots, none of which I ever saw again!

For many years my boy supported his wife, concubine, three children, and the wife and family of his eldest son, all living in the servant's quarters, together with an old gentleman, the latter evidently paying him for board and lodging—and all of them consuming nourishment provided by me under the deluded impression that I and my family simply had a good hearty appetite!

He must have made the equivalent of at least a hundred a year sterling out of me, over and above his wages, which were $25 (£2 10s.) a month, from which, theoretically he was supposed to pay for his own food. His wife, who did the washing, received $18 (£1 16s.) and she also helped to look after the children.

Every now and again he came to me and said, with a bland smile, 'Master, my wantchee go way littee time. My grandmother [or uncle, or cousin] have makee die!' He then went away for an enjoyable opium debauch of a couple of weeks or so! Of course, when I came to know his real nature I gave him a holiday for good and all. I discharged him with a bonus of $250, as in many ways he was a good boy, and, though he squeezed me himself, he never allowed anybody else to do so without giving him a good commission. He asked me for $1,500 to buy a laundry, and was rather surprised when I declined. Many Chinese give food and no pay to their servants, which seems to me a good way out of all trouble.

One day I was accused by my boy of growing opium, which is against the laws of China. The police had noticed a border of small Iceland poppies in the garden and had asked that we should uproot them. We did so!

The young bachelor often has a distaste for the coventions ordaining exactly what he should do and say under all circumstances. One of the first duties of a newcomer is to call on the various members of his office staff and their wives. This was contemptuously referred to in the Mess as 'poodle-faking'. As a young fellow of only nineteen I was rather diffident about this social obligation.

I have generally been most hospitably treated, and I trust I have done likewise to others. However, there have been exceptions, notably in the case of the stern housewife who was having tea, and did not offer me any, explaining that she never entertained; the Commissioner who reported me to the Head Office in Peking as 'socially unpresentable' because I did not call sufficiently often; and another, who sent me away because his wife did not receive until after dark. In the last case I called later, as directed, and came to the conclusion that my hostess, being rather plain, certainly looked less forbidding 'in the dark with a light behind her'! By the way, she never wore stockings, which, we thought, must have been a treat for the mosquitoes.

I once set out to visit one of our shining lights, and was told he was in the Club, so I went there, to find him. On inquiry I discovered he was at the top of a high pillar in the bar-room, and I was informed that, after a certain number of drinks, if a man wants another one, he has to satisfy the company as to his sobriety by climbing a pillar and touching the ceiling. 'And if he doesn't touch it?' I asked. 'He *always* does,' was the reply; 'we all help him!'

It is the general rule in China to keep open house to all and sundry, and if the host is not at home his boy will entertain the guest with drinks and smokes. From time to time I have been visited by passing strangers who say, 'I heard of you in Canton [or Wuchow, or Nanning, or some other place]. Can you put me up for a day or two?' I usually told them I should have to raise the salary of my publicity agent, but being really quite good-natured, I did not allow them to seek the shelter of the local Chinese inn, with its innumerable insects and general lack of sanitation. I found many of these visitors quite interesting, with a few exceptions, for instance when two adventurers, one Dutch and the other Italian, with no money and no luggage, came to stay, apparently for good, and ran up a pretty hefty bill at the Club for drinks, for which they signed 'chits', giving my name as a responsible reference. After some time I bought them a couple of steamer tickets, which they accepted with regret. There was also the case of the morphia addict, who was equally difficult to speed on his way.

A man once called and informed me that as my name is Williams, and as he was actually travelling for Dr Williams's Pink Pills, he thought he would take the liberty of availing himself of my hospitality! There being some humour in this ingenious suggestion, I took him in. He 'sat at my humble board and ate of my frugal store', and I found him quite entertaining. In response to inquiry he told me the famous pills sold at a very good profit. 'Well,' I remarked, 'in that case, perhaps, like Beecham's Pills, they are worth a guinea a box, and you ought to raise the declared value for payment of Customs Import Duty!' I asked him if his sales were good.

'Yes,' he replied, 'the Chinese buy them in large quantities, because they have great confidence in them. The only drawback is that they think one can never have too much of a good thing, so they take too many at once, as in the case of their own herbal remedies.' I asked him if he kept mortality statistics covering the various localities he visited. 'Oh, no,' he answered, 'I just move on as soon as I have made my sales!'

A ginrickshaw (*lit.*: man's strength carriage) was very useful to go calling in. I used to hire one, with a coolie to pull it, for fifteen dollars a month. One day I had an economical idea. I bought a rickshaw and hired the coolie for only twelve dollars. Then he began to be late, and the rickshaw would disappear for hours on end. I finally discovered he was letting it out on hire in my absence. Now he began to be careless. He ran into everything and everybody, and broke a wheel off the affair, but nobody would buy the pieces, so I had to invest in a new vehicle. The first day I went out, the coolie's hat blew off, and he jumped into the air to catch it, but could not come down again, and remained in the air, clinging to the shafts, while I was reclining on my back holding on chiefly with my feet! At the same time we were all rapidly tobogganing down a steep hill. There was no back to the rickshaw when we reached the bottom, and there was no coolie either, because he evidently thought discretion was the better part of valour, and decided to leave me to sort myself out from the wreckage. He returned the following morning with his own rickshaw, full of smiles, hoping that I had learned my lesson, and would now employ him in the normal way—but I decided to walk in future!

As a young man, I have lived in messes where, on the occasion of a birthday or festival, some of us were unable to hold our liquor successfully, though others, with hollow legs, seem to get away with it all right. One young fellow insisted on going to bed in the dog-kennel, after a jovial dinner-party, and remained there until the next morning, when his Chief went to find him. Then he put his head out and barked! A lecture was given to the Mess by the Chief against the evils of drinking. A few days later the Mess invited him to tiffin, the garden paths being carefully edged with numerous beer-bottles, through which he had to walk with some care. He did not refer, however to this unusual form of garden decoration. The bottles, which had been borrowed from the compradore, or grocer, for the purpose, were then returned. So honour was satisfied!

In Chinkiang, in the old days, it used to be said: 'There are three tanks in this town; the Standard Oil Tank, the Asiatic Petroleum Tank, and old Tank George!' Such was George's reputation. Like Prince Ma of the T'ang dynasty, he was merely an animated wine-skin, and, in the same manner as the great poet Li T'al-po, he finally

met his end by drowning when leaning out of a boat in the attempt
to embrace the reflection of the moon in the water—that 'fair maiden
with white fire laden'. A truly artistic finish!

Trade was good in Hankow in 1903. The Russian tea merchants
were very prosperous. When the Keemun and other teas were
gathered they went to Kiukiang to buy them, and they were blended
and shipped from Hankow. The Russians kept open house to all.
Money meant nothing to them. They were great gamblers and
played poker without any limit, except the sky. I have seen a card
table piled two or three feet high with paper money during the
course of a game!

There was a Mr Panoff whom I knew. One day I noticed, posted
up on the Club notice-board, that he had won the Champions Sweepstake, a very large sum of money, being the premier prize in the race-
meeting. I met him in the street and congratulated him. He had not
heard about it. 'Well,' he casually remarked, 'I thought from your
excited manner that you were going to tell me something *important*!'

I went for a drive with a Mr Popoff in his new Victoria carriage,
drawn by two fine imported Australian whalers (there were no cars
then). On the way we passed a rather beautiful Russian lady. He
stopped and raised his hat. 'What a lovely carriage, and what
magnificent horses!' she declared. 'They're yours,' he said, and,
jumping out of the carriage, he handed her the reins. She accepted.
I thought I had better get out, though I should rather have liked to
stay in the carriage, which was very nice, and so was the lady. But
I had no courage.

'Come to the Club,' said Mr Popoff. At the Russian Club we met
Mr Voronsky, who challenged Mr Popoff to shake dice for a thousand
dollars. 'Of course,' said Mr Popoff, who won the money and bought
himself another carriage and pair with it!

We had a Russian staying with us in our Mess for a time. He was
a noted chess-player, having represented Russia in the world
championship. I was the only player, so I was put forward to play
against him. He was winning hand over fist, when I suddenly
noticed, by chance, an opening for a checkmate, so I won the game.
He was very much surprised and most complimentary. He wanted
to recommend me for presidency of the local chess club. He asked
me how I worked out my theory of play, and asked me to play again.
I thanked him, declined the presidency, and begged to be excused
another game. I preferred to rest on my unexpected laurels!

Another Russian guest had an extraordinary capacity for vodka, but sometimes it affected his head. We played a joke on him one night, and when he was asleep we decorated the outside of his mosquito-net with artificial insects, spiders, scorpions, beetles, etc., which the Chinese make very skilfully out of silk. In the morning we heard loud groans. 'Tell me,' he gasped, 'are those real?'

'No,' we replied, quite truthfully.

'Well, give me another glass of vodka, and they may disappear!' he said, in a horrified tone of voice.

In my early days there was a craze among the younger generation for collecting souvenirs. The rooms of some of my bachelor friends were hung with such objects as shop-signs, fittings from railway-carriages, steamers and hotels, together with crockery and cutlery 'collected' from various public establishments. One genius exhibited with pride a tailor's dummy! The commandeering of these articles became a sort of cult.

One night I dined at a Shanghai restaurant known as the 'Owl Grill' with two such connoisseurs, and one of them, despite my gentle protests, insisted upon purloining the plated milk-jug. After dinner we saw him off on a steamer, but, unfortunately, he fell into the water between the pontoon and the vessel. With the help of a sampan (small boat) we fished him out—but he seemed very sad and gloomy.

'Cheer up,' we urged, 'you might have been drowned!'

'That's all very well,' he moaned, 'but I've *lost the milk-jug!*'

I often look back to the amusing times I had in those old cosmopolitan bachelor messes. We certainly were a motley crew. The German, who kept his dogs in his bath; the Japanese, who sat, cross-legged, in silent contemplation; the American, who 'skinned' us all at poker; the Frenchman who never changed his collar; the Belgian, who was always in love. But, somehow or other, we managed to pull together—anyhow, more successfully than the League of Nations!

At most of the ports there was a Customs Club, with one or more billiard tables, and billiard tournaments were frequently arranged. I remember reaching the finals of one such contest, but I lost it, as my opponent *would* insist on turning somersaults, standing on his head, and behaving generally like a clown during the game, which was rather disconcerting, to say the least of it, though not in any way contrary to the rules of the Billiard Association. On looking up his service record in the office, I found that before joining the outdoor

Staff of the Customs he had been a comedian and bandmaster! Incidentally, one of his accomplishments was the production of very tuneful melodies by passing his fingers down a number of billiard cues of different weights and lengths. He was, in fact, a very good billiard player!

There was plenty of outdoor recreation as well. The Americans and Japanese concentrated chiefly on baseball. The British played cricket, football, hockey, tennis, and golf. Hai-alai, or pelote Basque, a kind of glorified fives, was played by Continental professionals, and the onlookers gambled on the results.

In the north of China the golfing greens are brown, for they are made of rolled mud, and if it rains they are sometimes washed away altogether! Grass only grows well in the central and southern provinces. I played golf at Peking some years ago, when the Chinese war-lords Chang Tso-lin (afterwards assassinated) and Wu P'ei-fu (who later retired to a monastery) were carrying on a certain amount of desultory warfare, and some of the troops involved were encamped on the golf-course. At one point of the fairway there were some old railway-cars, occupied by soldiers engaged in preparing their midday meal near by. I asked my opponent, 'What club do I use for this shot?' 'A niblick,' he replied. I thereupon attempted to 'loft' my ball over these unnatural hazards. Unfortunately the ball fell into an iron pan of sizzling hot vegetable soup, so I claimed a rub on the green! At that moment an irate warrior picked out the ball from the stew, cursing loudly as he burnt his fingers, and threw it away. It landed on the green, and I went down in two under par, which was rather surprising, as the ball seemed to have become rather bulgy in parts owing to the temporary cooking it had received *en route*!

In 1932, the manager of a British bank in Harbin, Manchuria, was having a pleasant game of golf with his assistant when they were suddenly attacked by bandits who clubbed them with their own golf-sticks! Fortunately they escaped before they encountered any other dangerous traps on the course!

I once heard of an ingenious gentleman who invented a kind of harness made of metal springs, which he wore inside his clothes in order to ensure his swinging the golf-club correctly when making a stroke. He creaked and fell about just like the White Knight in *Alice in Wonderland*! He had only one club with an adjustable head, which could be used as anything between a putter and a driving-iron. When playing billiards he also used a cue of which the end could be detached if the tip came off, and he would produce a spare tipped end from his waistcoat pocket. Once there were some riots in Shanghai, due to a disputed decision in the Mixed Court, and he came to the office armed with a combined revolver, dagger, and knuckle-duster all in one! Thus he was well provided with all the necessary equipment for any kind of game!

Hong Kong and Shanghai were often visited by various touring theatrical and opera companies, but, owing to changing conditions and the competition of the cinema, etc., they do not now go there so often. Some of the 'barn-stormers' at the old Lyceum Theatre at Shanghai gave blood-curdling performances. At one melodrama, I remember the villain had lured the heroine to a lonely cottage, and offered her a cup of drugged coffee. 'Drink it,' he said, with a wicked leer; 'it will do you so much good!' She took it in her hand, and was just about to raise it to her lips, when, suddenly a young lady sitting near me in the audience stood up and screamed out: 'Don't drink it, *don't* drink it!' This created great amusement—even to the 'villain'.

I have attended a good many fancy-dress dances and skating carnivals in China. For one dance I shaved my head and dressed as a Buddhist priest. It was tremendously hot, and I remember how delightful it was when I returned home in the 'wee sma' hours' and had a cold shower-bath on my bald pate. I have won prizes as Robin Hood and the King of the Cannibal Islands. In the latter costume I was profusely decorated with large bones, which I obtained from the butcher, and painted white. I have also appeared successfully in Chinese costume, when I had a long conversation with a certain British Consul, who actually thought I was Chinese. I have been to children's parties in some of these dresses, and, of course, have officiated as Father Xmas. At one of these gatherings the dear little kiddies gave *me* a present—it was MUMPS!

At a variety show in Shanghai, Sandow appeared with a troupe of strong men of different nationalities, including Chinese. They were challenged to wrestle against a team of Japanese, who were giving an exhibition at the same time at the Changsuho Gardens, but as Sandow's men knew nothing of ju-jitsu they came off rather badly. However, Sandow rippled his muscles to music very effectively, while standing on a revolving pedestal. There was also a Chinese conjurer, who was booed so much that he realized he was a frost, so he announced that he would conclude his performance by making a dragon appear on the stage. He made his exit drawing a rope behind him. The rope continued trailing across the stage until eventually a small chicken was seen at the other end. Thus the audience got the bird instead. The conjurer got away with the box-office receipts! Really a very good disappearing trick!

Nature is sometimes generous; at other times she is destructive, and visits whole districts with floods, earthquakes, and typhoons. Some years ago I was resting on a long cane chair on the veranda of the Hong Kong Hotel, when the chair travelled steadily from one end of the veranda to the other owing to an earthquake. At the same time part of the hotel fell down!

On another occasion, when I was stationed in Shanghai, the electric ceiling fans in the office began swaying about alarmingly for the same reason, and one of them dropped with a loud crash on the export desk! One of my colleagues even declared that the pictures in his house stood out almost at right angles to the wall—and remained in that position for some time! I was almost inclined to believe him, but he was Irish!

Shanghai presented a most Venetian appearance during the great typhoon of 1905, the streets being mostly three or four feet deep in flood water. The tide rushed in very suddenly from the river, and a considerable amount of damage was done. A certain Chinese merchant remarked to me over the counter of the office: 'Anything belong vellee bad just now! First have got Amellican boycott, no can buy, no can sellum all Amellican thing; then have got silver dollar plice no good; and today catchee largee typhoon, anyside too muchee water, allee sugar inside my go-down allo-same sit down!'

The Racecourse was a lake, and some fish had got into it from some neighbouring stew-ponds, so I went out there and helped to catch them with drag-nets. While doing this I got badly sunburnt all over, as I only had shorts on. Telegraph poles, etc., were floating about in the roads, with enterprising Chinese in pursuit; men and women were navigating logs of wood, others improvised rafts, and sculled about in wooden wash-tubs, etc. It was not only the biggest storm on record for Shanghai, but it also created great havoc among the shipping all round the coast, and especially at Hong Kong, where whole steamers were thrown up on the rocky shores!

When I was in Peking, the Chinese Government instituted a National State Lottery for the purpose of raising funds for the construction of aeroplanes and motor roads, and, in the hope of attracting

叙

本月八日（星期三）下午四時歡送

英國公使藍博森治茗候

故宮博物院代理院長馬 衡謹訂

座設咸福宮

*The Director
of the Palace Museum
cordially invites you to a tea reception
to bid farewell to
H. E. Sir Miles W. Lampson,
H. B. M. Minister to China,
and to view a special exhibition of
Chien-Lung's autographs and other treasures
on Wednesday, 8th November, at the Hsier Fu Kung,
Palace Museum, at four o'clock.*

Entrance from Shen Wu Men.

Invitation to a reception in the Palace Museum, Peking, to bid
farewell to Sir Miles Lampson, H.B.M.'s Minister, 1934

Country Life, Nanking, 1909

foreign capital, advertised in the English and French newspapers as follows: 'Hope is the essence of life. Without hope life is empty. Be human therefore and live in hope. You have just as much chance of drawing one of the big prizes in the State Lottery as any other person. Therefore buy a ticket with confidence and hope!'

China is a great gambling country and is inundated with advertisements of foreign lotteries as well. I once received one which ran: 'Richard the First offered his kingdom for a horse. *We* offer you a horse for only sixpence!' Foreign sweepstakes, with their fabulous prizes in millions of pengos, pesetas, milreas, or whatnot, are certainly most attractive. But, even if you win, as the Chinese say: 'Money is dissipated as easily as the shell of an egg.' Thus leaving us exactly where we were before.

Good fortune comes to some people while they are asleep. One morning I was awakened and a telegram was handed to me reading: 'Congratulations you have won hundred pounds Irish sweepstake do nothing until further instructions.' I was too surprised to do anything! Five minutes later I received another telegram: 'Operation appendicitis necessary for son wire one hundred pounds immediately.' In my bath I sang in a mournful voice. But I soon cheered up. After all, my accounts were balanced. Eventually it turned out that the operation was successful and only cost seventy pounds, so I was thirty pounds to the good, which I invested in the races, lost it all— and won it back again!

The China pony of the Manchurian plains, with the jockey's legs protruding on each side of him, and reaching almost as far as the ground, cuts a very funny figure; but year after year the little communities of foreigners in the treaty ports manage to coax him to race round a track, so that they may back him to win. Nearly everybody attends the races, the men chiefly as a business speculation, the ladies to outdo each other in the 'creations' of their milliners.

The last race-meeting I attended was a very good one—at least, so everybody else said. During the few days that the races last, people are in a veritable fever of excitement; all expect to win large sums of money, and it usually turns out that the wealthiest are heavy winners, while from the poor unfortunates is taken all that which they previously possessed. I once noticed an exception to this general rule, when a shabby old gentleman won so much money that it was all he could do to carry it away. Sad to relate, he died of overexcitement, aggravated by drink, a few days later!

The evening before each race-day, selling lotteries are held at the various clubs, in which vague speculations are made and much money is sunk, sometimes to rise up two or three times, like a drowning man, and finally disappear, and, less frequently, to multiply itself and return a handsome dividend.

I bought a horse in Peking, and persuaded a friend to ride him in the races, but he did not even cover the cost of his keep, and so I sold him at a loss. Then he began to win!

The old 'China hands' were very fond of entertaining. I had the pleasure of meeting Mr and Mrs Archibald Little at a dinner-party when I was a bachelor in Hankow in 1904.

They were interesting people. Mr Little was known as the Pioneer of the Yangtze Gorges, being the first man to get a steamer up to Chungking. He was the author of several standard books on the geography and geology of the Far East. Mrs Little was also a well-known novelist, with a strong sense of humour. I sat next to her. She whispered to me, 'Lend me your pumps for a minute!' I took them off and handed them to her under the table, wondering what she wanted them for.

She put them on her knees, with the toes projecting over the edge of the table. Then she leaned over and said to her *vis-à-vis*, 'Excuse me, Mr Blenkinsop, but would you mind taking your feet *off my lap*!'

Later on she asked me, 'Who do you get to darn your socks?' This was rather an embarrassing question, but I merely replied, 'My boy's wife.' Some young students were in the habit of employing what was commonly known as a 'sleeping dictionary', a point which Mrs Little brought out in her tales of the China ports.

Lord Kitchener visited Nanking when I was stationed there in 1910. He was lavishly entertained by Chinese and British officials. The Viceroy H. E. Chang Chih-tung invited him to a banquet and asked him to choose any object from his extensive collection of Chinese works of art. Kitchener was, of course, a great collector himself, and he took great pleasure in selecting a very fine piece of Nanking blue china.

The British Consul gave a large reception for him, and showed him, with great pride, an enormous porcelain vase, which stood in a corner of the drawing-room. 'Turn it upside down,' said Kitchener, 'and let me see the marks.' It was very heavy and two coolies lifted it out for his inspection. He took a magnifying-glass from his pocket and examined the marks on the base. Then he pronounced judgement. 'Imitation!' he declared briefly.

The Consul was very disappointed, as he had paid a very large sum of money for the vase, which he had intended to present to Lord Kitchener. Needless to say, he did not make the presentation under the circumstances.

By keeping one's eyes and ears open, it is possible to find out quite a lot of what is going on all around, and this may be partly the secret of the Chinese 'bush telegraph' as operated by the native. From time to time my Customs salary, rightly or wrongly, was increased, and, of course, it was the business of my boy to see that my domestic expenditure should rise in equal proportion, thus increasing his own commission. Sometimes I received news of these promotions from my boy, even before I had any official intimation myself. He would say to me: 'Master catchee more wages now.' 'How do you know?' I ask. 'My savee. Any man talkee you belong more big. I think so more better you allo same pay me more money now!'

Of course, I had to! But I have heard of a man who lost his job and his boy refused to take any wages until his master obtained other employment. Then he asked for his back pay!

CHAPTER 17

Traditional Cathay

'Cathay' is the name given by the well-known Venetian traveller Marco Polo to the northern part of China, because that was the name of the ruling people in that district during the tenth century. Tennyson's line: 'Better fifty years of Europe than a cycle of Cathay', is rather misleading. He evidently pictured a cycle as being an extremely long period of time, whereas it is actually only sixty years, in China, and has been since it was invented by a gentleman called Ta Nao in the twenty-seventh century B.C.

Then again is Tennyson's analogy entirely accurate? From my own experience of rather more than half a cycle in the country, I should be inclined to disagree. Life in Europe has not been absolutely ideal during the last cycle—neither in war nor in peace—and there is much to be said for the care-free existence I usually enjoyed, far away from the hurly-burly of so-called civilization.

The foreign conception of China and its people is entirely wrong. First and foremost it is an exploded idea that the Chinese are anti-foreign. They are nothing of the kind. They are not opposed to foreigners at all. They are merely opposed to interference by foreigners in the even tenor of their existence. They believe in a policy of live and let live. They are proud of their old history, and consider themselves the moral equal, if not superior, to any other people.

The Chinese have somehow acquired the reputation of being a strange nation, with a peculiar language, curious institutions, manners and customs, utterly distinctive from those of Western countries. This has been largely true in the past, chiefly owing to the fact that for many centuries China was segregated from the rest of the world, and naturally developed along her own lines. But, after the country was thrown open to foreign trade and relations, certain modifications began to be adopted, until now it may be said that, in all essential points, China is just as civilized as any other country would be under similar circumstances.

Indeed, in many respects her people are even more civilized than we are. For instance, they know more about the art of living than we do. They are always happy even if they are poor. They are the only people who are gifted with a perfect repose. No others have the faculty of relaxation developed to such a fine degree. They fully appreciate the subtle enjoyment of indefinite procrastination, and of remaining for lengthy periods in a blissful state of total inaction!

They are a simple and philosophical people. They have the greatest admiration for a person who has what they call 'a hollow bamboo in the heart'. In making a bamboo water-pipe, the sections are cut out. When the heart is open a man has no foregone conclusions nor prejudices. He is honest and straightforward. We may trust him implicitly. He will not be stupid nor narrow-minded. In fact, his mind will be open to argument and compromise, but it will be active and efficient.

The superstitions of the Chinese were rather a drawback to general progress in the past, but the higher classes are now more enlightened. The building of early railways was much impeded by 'feng-shui', a belief in geomantic influences which prevented interference with the contour of the countryside. Unnecessary tunnels and bridges are to be seen on certain railways, having been constructed to allow for the free circulation of the 'feng-shui'.

The foreigner experiences a quaint fascination for the picturesque unexpectedness to be found in the course of the daily life of the natives. In certain respects he finds them rather incongruous until he realizes that, in many ways, the people are really quite logical. These differences would probably strike him as unusual, for instance:

FOREIGN STYLE	CHINA FASHION
We write from left to right.	They write from right to left.
We write horizontally.	They write vertically.
We date: 1 May 1948.	They date: 1948 May 1.
To count on the fingers we close the hand and open finger by finger.	They open the hand first and then close finger by finger.
When we make an addition we commence with the simple units and finish with the higher figures.	With them the process is reversed.

Our women wear low-cut gowns.

Theirs have high collars.

Our women restrict their waists.

Theirs bind in the breast.

With us a woman may figuratively wear the trousers.

With them she actually does.

We undress to go to bed.

They sleep in their clothes.

With us the colour of mourning is black.

With them it is white.

At meals we begin with soup and end with fruit.

They begin with fruit and end with soup.

We have a plate each.

They eat from the same dish.

We have large tumblers which we do not refill very often.

They have small ones which they refill immediately after drinking.

We drink with our food and, smoke after.

They drink before and after, and smoke at meals.

We bathe before a meal.

They bathe after.

We like cool drinks in summer.

They like hot tea in the warmest weather.

We like ripe fruits.

They prefer them unripe.

We eat quietly.

They eat noisily to show their appreciation.

We eat with the family at the same table.

With them males and females eat separately.

We drink tea on arrival at a visit.

They drink it on departure.

We like to walk abreast.

They walk in single file.

When riding we put our toes in the stirrups.

They place their heels in the stirrups.

We carry babies in our arms.

They tie them on their backs.

We cut our nails short.

They keep them as long as possible (as a sign of distinction, or to show that they have no need to work).

We use our handkerchiefs.

They consider them ridiculous and unpleasant.

With us a man adopts a son.

With them a child adopts a father.

Our students face the master in class.	Theirs turn their backs when repeating their lessons.
With us the place of honour is the right.	With them it is the left.
We say: You and I.	They say: I and you.
We say: Ancient and modern.	They say: Modern and ancient.
We say: North, south, east, west.	They say: East, south, west, north.
We say: To go on board a ship.	They say: To go down into a ship.
We say: Coming and going.	They say: Going and coming.
We say: Cover up your head.	They say: Cover up your stomach.
We put flowers on graves.	They put food on them.
We shake hands with a friend.	They shake their own hands.
Some of us say we are descended from monkeys.	They say that monkeys have descended from *them*!

If a Chinese marries and has no children, he either tries to persuade some youth to join his family or else his wife applies to the local quack for some kind of charm which is supposed to induce the birth of a child. It is considered important to have a son, so that he may worship at the tomb of his father, thereby securing peace and comfort to the soul of the deceased in the other world.

I heard of a case when a barren woman asked a fortune-teller to provide her with the necessary charm. He told her that 'the dragon was sucking her blood!' But he could give her a good charm for eight dollars. This charm, he explained, would be made from blood extracted from the toes of a lizard, a tortoise, and a stork, and she was instructed to sleep with it under her pillow! History does not relate whether it had the desired effect or not.

One of my Chinese clerks in the office told me that his wife had given birth to a daughter that morning. I congratulated him, and asked him how many children he had altogether. 'Five,' he replied, 'all girls.' As it is polite to refer to a daughter as 'a thousand pieces of gold', I said, 'Well, now you are very rich, as you have five thousand pieces of gold!' He was evidently suffering from *embarras de richesses*.

The ideal Chinese family is three sons and two daughters, five being a lucky number. A picture of a *Ch'i-lin*, a fabulous monster something like a unicorn, is often hung up in a Chinese house, and believed to induce childbirth, on the analogy that the mother of Confucius is said to have conceived her famous son when treading in the footmarks of that auspicious animal.

Chinese children usually have two names. The first is the 'milk name', which is used during the years of childhood, and possibly later as a term of endearment by the family. The second is the family surname, together with one, or more, generally two personal names. A child is often given a derogatory name, such as 'Little Slave' for a girl, or 'Bald-head' for a boy, or even the name of an animal such as 'Ox', 'Pig', etc., in the belief that the evil spirits will not trouble to interfere with children possessing such insignificant names. A parent may also name his child according to the time or place of his birth, his hopes of prosperity, or love of beauty and poetry. Girls may be called Flower, Lucky Pearl, Precious Harp, or Bright Spring; and boys can be named Dog, Flea, Fragrant Palace, or Learned Treatise.

A Chinese soothsayer once told my fortune by the stars, the mystic diagrams of the 'Book of Changes', by phrenology, palmistry, and also by the lines on the soles of my feet! I thought I might as well have the whole bag of tricks. He promised me an enormous number of children, all of whom would rise to great eminence. He also declared that, according to my left hand, I ought to be dead already, as my line of life is broken in the middle; however, it is nicely joined together in my right hand and left foot, and, moreover, there appears to be no end to it at all. So he said I would live for ever!

China may appear to be a land of paradoxes, and often the occidental finds it rather difficult to follow the many inverted customs of the country. But the fact that the Chinese will frequently do something in a manner entirely opposite to that of a foreigner does not necessarily indicate that they are wrong—either of them. *Chaque pays chaque moeurs.* There are two sides, moreover, to every question.

At an official dinner-party at Peking there were present, among others, the Chinese Minister of Finance, and the Commercial Attaché of a certain Legation. The latter said to the former, 'Many people ask me how it is that China is always in financial difficulties at the end of each fiscal year, and yet she always pulls through and goes on happily for another year. Can you explain this?'

The Chinese Minister smiled and replied, 'The next time anybody asks you, just tell him that China is a magical country, and we do it by magic!' The Chinese never fail to see a joke, nor to find their way out of a difficulty.

Dr Wellington Koo, at a diplomatic dinner, sat next to an American gentleman who inquired cheerfully of this Chinese Ambassador, 'Likee soupee?' Later on Dr Koo rose and made an excellent speech in faultless English. When he resumed his seat, amid great applause, he asked his neighbour, 'Likee speechee?'

Time passes slowly in the East and seems to be of no account whatsoever. Everybody moves deliberately, and with extreme dignity. There is no rushing to catch trains, no fixed time for anything. Clocks and watches are all different, being affected, no doubt, by the sudden climatic changes. Punctuality is certainly not a Chinese virtue, and procrastination is never regarded as the thief of time. Shakespeare's warning that 'time and tide wait for no man' does not apply in China. There is plenty of time, and you can always wait for the tide, or stay for the next one.

In spite of the general habit of ignoring the time, however, the Chinese are passionately fond of clocks. The Emperor had a large collection of them in the Forbidden City. They were of different kinds, some most beautiful and ingenious, with mechanical figures of human beings, birds and animals, and every imaginable sort of striking bell and chime. To hear them all striking twelve at once was a wonderful experience. There were also musical boxes, whistling models of birds, etc., in great variety. One figure of a man actually wrote Chinese characters with a brush-pen when he was wound up.

The Chinese are very keen on pomp and ceremony, especially the poorer classes, in whose life there is little colour. Processions are important in the daily life of the people. Wedding processions, funeral processions, and processions to the temples, are often to be seen. Those taking part are elaborately costumed and carry banners and lanterns, though such paraphernalia is merely hired as required, as also are the wedding presents, very often, when carried to the bridegroom's house.

What are the Chinese but a vast procession themselves? They are as the sands of the sea, and are tending to increase still further. Very likely the number of Chinese in the whole world, i.e. not only those in China proper, but also in Mongolia, Tibet, Manchuria, Malaysia, the Philippines, America, etc., would amount to quite 600,000,000. If they could all be assembled into one vast procession, four abreast, and marching fifteen miles a day at the rate of three miles an hour, they would require about twenty-three years, or one generation, to pass a given point, as 26,280,000 would pass every year. If we may assume that the birth-rate is ten per cent, and half the children die before they can walk, there would be 30,000,000 more Chinese every year to replace the 26,280,000 who have passed the given point. Thus the procession, like the soul of the celebrated John Brown, would for ever 'go marching on'! Which reminds me that I have heard 'John Brown's Body' played at both weddings and funerals in China.

Walking, as an exercise, in point of fact, does not appeal to the Chinese at all, and they cannot understand why on earth anybody should take so much trouble, since transportation by sedan chairs or rick-shaws is so cheap and convenient. I was in the habit of taking a walk every day at Lungchow, for the good of my health, along the Ta Ma Lu, or Great Horse Road, leading out of the town, and was often challenged by soldiers on patrol duty, who were suspicious of my motives in walking abroad in such an unusual manner!

I asked a Chinese official once if he played tennis. 'No,' he replied, 'but it seems an interesting game; I shall tell my coolie to play, and then I shall be able to watch him, sitting comfortably in the shade!' In modern times, however, the Chinese students have taken up football and tennis to some extent.

Ball games such as polo and football were popular in China about a thousand years ago and then gradually went out of fashion. The football was originally made of bamboo, and the game was merely a kind of acrobatic spectacle of a non-competitive nature. It concluded by kicking the ball between two goalposts decorated with flowers. During the Sung dynasty a football player called Yoo Chew was presented at Court and eventually rose to the position of Prime Minister. This may have been the goal of his ambition, but, owing to his general mismanagement of national affairs, he was soon kicked out of it again!

Bret Harte's assertion that 'the heathen Chinee is peculiar' was, of course, a subtle jest, but it is often quoted as an axiom, and so it needs debunking. Firstly, he is not well defined as a heathen. There is not much in Confucianism which is really contrary to Christianity —and, by the way, how many true Christians are there? Confucius would have been very popular in England. Good form in its English sense, the achievement of what is proper and fitting, was his chief desideratum.

Our golden rule, 'Do unto others what you would others do unto you', certainly becomes, in the Confucian teaching, 'Do *not* unto others what you would *not* others do unto you', but this is only a distinction without a difference—passive instead of active.

Buddhism, in its original purity, is a highly moral code, and should definitely be approved by the Society for Prevention of Cruelty to Animals, though it must be admitted that it now has an admixture of Lama and Taoist animism. There is, however, much poetry and love of Nature in Taoism.

Secondly, the inhabitant of the Celestial Kingdom is not a Chinee, nor a Chink; nor should he be called John Chinaman. He hates all these derogatory nicknames, and prefers to be called a man of T'ang, a son of Han, or simply a Chinese.

Thirdly, he does not consider himself in any way 'peculiar', though he might possibly apply that epithet to us, in certain cases, if he were not so polite. The vast majority of the Chinese people are not the crafty schemers of complicated mentality, as commonly believed by the average Occidental. They are a pleasant, simple and hard-working people, consisting chiefly of agriculturalists—the finest in the world.

The foreign conception of the personal appearance of the Chinese is also almost invariably incorrect. He does not shuffle about in an odd manner, as in English musical comedy; neither does he wear, in the present day, embroidered robes and peacock's feathers. We used to wear a 'pig-tail', and so did he—but not now. That he has slanting eyes is a fallacy, for they are set in sockets as horizontal as our own; it is the eyebrows, growing upwards at a slightly acute angle, which have given rise to the popular belief. Take an average Chinese, and you will not find him ugly, furtive and leering; but handsome and graceful. And this also applies to his wife.

The late Mr G. K. Chesterton, that brilliant and versatile writer, made the following apposite remarks on Chinese affairs in the *Illustrated London News* of the 17th June 1933: 'The Japanese armies may advance today, over the land occupied by one of five rival Chinese generals yesterday. Tomorrow, both of them may have disappeared from practical politics; a national reaction may have restored the Son of Heaven to his sacred place in Pekin; or the Russian Communists may have swept across China and plotted it out under Commissars, that "the State" may start another Five-Year Plan. It is simply not possible for men to regard these tempestuous changes, in what the Chinese might call the Upper Air, as having the same relations to themselves as the mother that bore them, or the child that is born to them.'

The Chinese are chiefly concerned with gaining their livelihood, and, individually, pay little attention to political changes. China has sampled many different forms of government. She has been divided, in the past, into separate states warring one against another. She has been conquered several times by outlying tribes, which she has simply absorbed like a sponge. Slices of her territory have been cut off in the north and south. She has had Emperors, Regents and Presidents. For many years the National Party and the Communist Party have been in a continual state of civil war. The country has been laid waste and generally disrupted, not only by the Japanese, but by famine and floods. Nevertheless, the people have a natural gift of unlimited patience and indomitable industry and perseverance under great difficulties, so let us hope they will eventually develop a workable policy of general administration—fully acceptable to the whole nation.

Mediation between the rival parties, or intervention by foreign countries, will not solve the problem, for the Chinese will brook no interference; according to their saying from the 'Book of Odes', 'Brothers may contend against each other behind the walls of the city, but outside they join together to resist intruders.' They prefer to control their own policy with a free hand, and to work out their own salvation—even if progress is very slow. Perhaps a division of this great Middle Kingdom into Northern and Southern States, with a Central State Department, will be the eventual outcome. It is impossible to foretell the future.

Many foreigners have tried to explain the nature of the Chinese. But do the Chinese understand each other? Until they reach a definite understanding, and agree to 'bury the hatchet', in the interests of the State, the Nationalists and Communists will leave unsolved the great problem.

After a Japanese air-raid, a Chinese countryman, looking at the bomb-crater in his garden, remarked philosophically: 'This will make a very good fish-pond!' This seems to be the right spirit. Now is the time to make the best of things and bring the country back to normal. The Japanese menace is now removed, so let us hope the civil war will cease, and the energies of people may be directed towards making the best of the available resources of the Land of Cathay.

CHAPTER 18

With Gun and Dog

The ancient Chinese were highly skilled in the art of hunting. Archery and riding were considered the essential accomplishments of the gentry, and, as a great part of the country was undeveloped, the wild denizens of woods and fields were likely to become troublesome if not kept in check, and many were used as food.

The Emperor Fu Hsi (2953–2838 B.C.) was said to have been given his name, which means literally 'Hidden Victims', on account of the fact that he instructed his people how to snare birds and animals, and to secure the various products of the sea in nets.

It is recorded that Confucius was very fond of field sports such as archery and angling. He also applied his code of ethics to these things. He angled, but never fished with a net; he shot, but not at sitting birds.

Unlike Confucius, the modern Chinese does not take the risk of shooting game on the wing. He argues that if you shoot a bird in the air the shots are likely to spoil the breast, whereas if the bird is on the ground or in the water, it is only wounded in the back or the wing, and the flesh is not damaged for eating. He uses iron shot. I have broken several teeth on them, so I know! There is a common metaphor: '*Wang k'ung she yen*', 'to look up in the air while shooting a wild goose', which conjures up the picture of a man stupidly aiming his gun in the air in order to shoot a goose on the ground. This phrase is symbolical of extreme unreliability. It also proves that no Chinese (of modern days) ever dreams of shooting at a flying bird when he can make a dead certainty of it sitting, thus economizing in cartridges.

There is a good story illustrating the patience of the Chinese sportsman. He wanted to kill six ducks with one shot, and he therefore built a straw hut on the edge of a lake, and waited until six ducks were swimming in single file in the water. He had to watch for *sixty years* before this finally occurred. He fired and killed all the ducks, the bullet being found in the last duck! I heard this anecdote at a Chinese dinner-party, after the wine had circulated.

There is mention in Chinese records of the remarkable shooting of Kao P'ien, a courtier of the seventh century A.D., who was noted for having transfixed two eagles with one arrow, for which feat the Emperor gave him the title of 'Duke of the Double Eagle'.

The best archer in Chinese history was a man called Yi of the Hsia dynasty, 2205 B.C. He shot the Emperor and reigned in his stead until he was shot himself by one of his officers, who, up to that time, was the next best shot! Archery was a popular sport in those days, but they often preferred a living target, and the winner was always likely to be bumped off by the unsuccessful competitors!

The early Manchus were great hunters, and a vast tract of hundreds of miles, called the Wei Ch'ang, or Hunting Reserves, was set apart for preserving large game and exercising the Imperial troops in hunting. There the Emperor had his country palace and park, which were situated at Jehol one hundred miles north of Peking. The Emperor Ch'ien Lung, A.D. 1735, is said to have personally killed a tiger, which was stuffed and placed on exhibition in the Lama Temple at Peking, where I actually saw it—or at least the priests assured me it was the same animal; it looked very mangy, as nearly all the hair had fallen out, which is not surprising after a couple of hundred years!

In those days, the game was chiefly hunted with the aid of the Manchurian greyhound, and shot with bow and arrow. It was considered very lucky to bag a deer, as this animal was the emblem of happiness, longevity, and riches.

It is natural for man to engage in the pleasures of the chase. I come of an old Welsh family who supported King John against his rebellious barons, and as a reward he gave them an addition to their coat of arms, consisting of the device of a stag bearing the crown of England between its horns. This distinction carried with it the privilege of shooting the deer in the royal forests. So I suppose I may claim descent from a sporting stock. In any case I am glad to know that my progenitors had no necessity of stealing legs of beef!

History repeats itself, and so I eventually had the tacit approval of the Emperor of China to shoot the deer which roamed the forests and plains of his extensive dominions. Curiously enough the very first thing I ever shot in China was one of these animals, a specimen of the muntjac, or hog-deer, of the Yangtze valley. I had never had a gun in my hand before, but I was determined to bag something, if only to save my face. Suddenly I saw a bush, in the middle of a field, and it was shaking about in a peculiar manner. Perhaps there may be a tiger crouching behind ready to spring out on me, I thought. I took no chances and fired both barrels at the quivering bush, when out jumped a small stag, turned a somersault, and fell dead at my feet! Thus I followed the tradition of my sporting ancestry.

There was no restriction of any kind on shooting in China at that time, and I was not slow to avail myself of this healthy and attractive form of sport.

It was some time before I shot another stag, either by accident or on purpose, but I gradually acquired some skill. I never went in for piling up large bags, but only shot for the pot. Sometimes I have seen large parties proceeding into the countryside from the ports, who were out to slaughter any kind of animal or bird, whether edible or otherwise. These spoilsports should be prevented from depleting the fauna of the district simply for their own amusement.

China is decidedly a hunter's paradise, and game of all kinds is found in abundance, even in the neighbourhood of the towns. The Manchurian tiger is the largest in the world. The great panda is unique. The hills give shelter to a large variety of big game such as serow, goral, deer, and boar. On the lower slopes, and in the culti-vated plains, are numerous pheasant, partridge, quail, snipe and hare. In the lakes and marshes are innumerable flocks of duck, geese and other water-fowl. Carp and sturgeon are found in the rivers, and even alligators in the Yangtze.

The rough shooting of China, which is obtained by walking with dogs through the beautiful scenery, is far more enjoyable than our artificial method of sitting behind a specially constructed butt or shelter of turf, with a couple of loaders standing by alongside, ready to offer you a battery of shot-guns, and blazing away automatically at flocks of terrified birds driven overhead at regular intervals.

One of the most enjoyable recreations was to go upriver with some friends in a Chinese houseboat, and land on the bank in suitable country for the purpose of pheasant-shooting with the aid of a good sporting dog. On a fine winter's day it was a real joy to walk over hill and dale, and, when the dog came to a point, to wait for the upward rush of one or more game-birds, their plumage gay in the sun against the dark background of oak-scrub and bamboo.

I used to make my own cartridges, and, after some practice,

became a fairly good shot. I recall vividly my first effort in the winter
of 1903, when I set out from Hankow with my messmate K——, in
the Customs sailing lights tender *Fei Yun*. Travelling upriver during
the afternoon and evening, we anchored for the night at Kinkow.
The next morning we landed in good shooting country. K——
walked in front and I followed close behind him. Suddenly I tripped
up and my gun exploded. The shot passed within an inch of his leg.
It was as near as no matter—as they say in Yorkshire! 'Did you get
him?' he asked. 'No,' I replied, 'I just missed him!' Shortly after that
he fired at a quail, and immediately I felt a sharp blow on the side of my
head. 'You've shot me!' I shouted. Just then the wad of the cartridge
fell out of my shirt-collar. The wind had deflected it in my direction,
and it had struck me with some force, but without drawing blood.

When walking in thick cover it is necessary to take care to avoid
shooting a passing farmer or wood-cutter. I was out shooting once
with a novice who shot my hat off by mistake. This was his total bag
for the day, and he complained that I had had all the luck, I agreed!

I used to go out shooting with an old River Inspector in Hankow.
Before starting out in the early morning for the autumn snipe he
invariably put down a very strong dose of gin and bitters, and he
pressed me to join him in this refreshment. 'It's very kind of you,' I
said, 'but not so early in the day.'

'You're making a great mistake,' he declared; 'there's nothing like
having a good drink before you go out snipe-shooting, because a snipe
is a very small bird, but, after a good glass of gin, when it gets up it
looks as large as a turkey—and *you simply can't miss it!*' So saying he
poured himself out another dram with the well-known sailor's
excuse: 'A bird can't fly with only one wing.' That day he shot a
pelican. Perhaps he thought it was a snipe! But it probably looked
like a pterodactyl!

On another of my early shoots, with a couple of friends, three
pheasants suddenly whizzed up, in a beautiful bouquet, and I was so
lost in admiration that all I could do was to recall the lines of the
poet Pope:

> See from the brake the whirring pheasant springs,
> And mounts triumphant on exulting wings!

Shortly afterwards we all fired at a deer, which fell instantly, but, to
our amazement, turned out to be a domestic pig. We had to buy it.
Then we shot a rabbit, which changed into a cat. We bought that,

too! With loud honks a flock of wild geese passed overhead. We all fired and *I* shot a goose. At least that is my story and I stick to it!

I got a tiger once, and a much larger one than has ever been seen before. Some Chinese hunters from Manchuria had killed a tiger, and were offering the roughly cured skin in a raffle at Hankow in 1904. I won it. The reason why it was so large was because it had been stretched before curing, and in this way several inches had been gained, thus beating the record. They say you can always find a tiger by the smell. My visitors complained about this. So I sold the animal for fifteen pounds—before it went bad altogether!

As in the case of some fishermen, the gunner sometimes brags of his skill. I once met a Japanese out in the country. 'Have you shot anything?' I inquired.

'Oh, yes,' he replied, 'many kinds of animals and birds, but the dog he search all places and cannot find them!'

I once shot a Chinese peasant in the neck with one small pellet which had ricocheted from a tree. When I apologized he was very decent about it. I took the shot out with the point of my knife. The only other person I ever shot by mistake was a very fat Chinese woman who was bending down washing vegetables in a pond. My shooting-coolie handled the matter for me very expertly.

'Where have you been shot?' he inquired of her. 'Show me the place.' She refused to do this, so he said: 'Well, you can't prove it, then!' Actually she was wearing very thick wadded clothing, and, hit at sixty yards with small snipe-shot, which could not have penetrated, she only suffered a slight shock of dignity, which was immediately dispelled by the presentation of a silver dollar, one of the best forms of insurance against such incidents.

In the early days there were cases of Chinese villagers being accidentally killed by foreign sportsmen. Compensation of $100 per man to the family of the deceased was usually considered adequate. Nowadays it would be regarded as a very serious matter leading to international complications. Of course, there is no excuse for such gross carelessness.

At Kiukiang I often went for walks in the country with my gun. One afternoon during an hour's sport I secured a curious bag consisting of two hare, two pheasant, two mallard, two teal, two plover, two woodcock, and a brace of snipe.

Once I scared a pheasant to death. It was so disturbed at my approach that it rose and flew against a brick wall and dashed out its brains! A small Chinese boy picked it up and quickly ran into a house with it. I followed. The father of the family said he had seen no pheasant, but I noticed a trail of blood leading across the courtyard to an outhouse, so I proceeded to track it along. 'You can't go in there,' the old man exclaimed, 'it's my daughter's bedroom—and she's ill in bed!' I'm afraid I was not chivalrous (nor trustful) enough to agree, and so I went in—and there was the little boy *and* the pheasant!

Another curious bag I made one day was a brace of hare, a crested grebe, and *eight fish*! I got the fish in a strange way. Under the ice of a frozen pond I saw a number of carp, so I shot at them through the ice with No. 10 shot. The force of the charge made a hole in the ice and blew the water up in a kind of fountain, after which it rained fish, falling around me from the sky. They were quite stunned, which is not at all surprising!

There was an old-stager in Ningpo—a sort of Tartarin of Tarascon. He attired himself for shooting in a bottlegreen corduroy coat, two bandoliers of cartridges, an enormous shooting-bag slung on his back, blue dungaree trousers thrust into unwieldy hip-boots, the *tout ensemble* being crowned with a large yellow solar topee, like a tremendous mushroom, enfolded in a puggaree of many colours hanging down behind in a variegated festoon! He took with him a dog of doubtful ancestry, a very gun-shy animal, which invariably got lost, and was always more interested in other people's fowls than his master's birds. His bag was often quite large, but generally consisted of such inedible items as jays, crows, coots, and water-wagtails.

He loaded his own cartridges, using paper instead of felt wads. One day I was out with him when he fired at a marsh harrier, hovering overhead quite out of range. A large piece of newspaper fluttered out of the end of his gun and was wafted in my direction. I caught it and read: 'Forecast—North-east and easterly gale approaching rapidly; cloudy, with heavy showers of rain throughout the day.' 'I see by your latest *gun bulletin*,' I remarked, 'that we are in for a bad storm. I think we had better go home before we get caught in it!'

The following extract from one of my shooting-diaries will give a good idea of the China shooting:

31st December 1913. Leaving Ningpo by sedan-chair at 5 p.m., I arrived on board the houseboat at 5.45. My wife had come up in the boat. We reached Mo Tzu Yee Haulover at 8.45. This is an embankment plastered with wet mud to make it slippery so that boats can be

drawn over it with ropes into the higher level of the Ch'ien T'ang
Lake. Having overcome this obstacle, we proceeded to Ng Li Dong
Village, and moored alongside the causeway dividing the larger from
the smaller section of the lake. This causeway is a fine stone-faced
affair, about four hundred yards long. The small lake was under
process of dredging, and gangs of coolies were employed in burning
the reeds, digging the mud, and piling it up by the side of the causeway and the shores of the lake.

1st January 1914. I got up at 5 a.m. and went out into the large
lake, sitting in the bows of a small native punt covered with straw
and propelled by a coolie in the stern. The lake was frozen over to the
depth of about half an inch, and the ice had to be broken with a
bamboo pole to procure a free passage for the boat. Having tied up in
a conveniently situated clump of reeds, I very soon had a chance at a
passing teal, which I shot with the second barrel, following this up,
after reloading, with a shot at a big mallard, which fell with a broken
wing and had to be dispatched with the other barrel while it was
swimming away.

The flighting then continued until 7 a.m., immense flocks of duck
and teal coming over so that the sky was quite black with them. I
had eleven teal down, but only found eight, the rest having dived
among the interlaced roots of the reeds. Back to breakfast at 7.30,
and very hungry.

After breakfast we both went forth across the causeway, and began
climbing round the sides of the hills surrounding the lake, stopping
occasionally to admire the view and breathe the wonderful mountain
air. All of a sudden, with a rushing and a whirring, a fine cock pheasant flew out at my feet, and I dispatched it just as it was about to
disappear over the brow of the hill. After collecting a few botanical
specimens, we returned to the boat.

After tiffin I went out again on the lake and returned at tea-time
with four teal and a widgeon. At 5 p.m. we went together in the small
boats for the evening flight, and returned at six o'clock with three
mallard and a brace of teal, one of which was accounted for by my
wife with her 20-bore gun, and three more being lost owing to the
dusk.

2nd January 1914. My thirtieth birthday, which I started early by
going out flighting in the usual punt, acquiring three more teal and
a hearty appetite. After breakfast, the boat was moved across the lake
to Ossu, a place known also as Horseshoe Bend, a picturesque angle

of the lake. Here I landed and rambled about the hills during the morning, bringing back a brace of squirrels with grey backs and red chests, which I wanted for inclusion in a museum of stuffed birds and animals I had formed in the Campo Club, Ningpo, of which I was Honorary Secretary.

After tiffin the lake was recrossed, but progress was slow, as there was a strong headwind. We then went out on the hills behind Ng Li Dong Village, and afterwards sallied forth in the punts for the evening flight, from which I brought back three teal.

3rd January 1914. Only two or three more cartridges left! I went out for the early flight, lost one teal but secured another. The total bag for the whole trip was exactly thirty head, comprising: twenty-two teal, four mallard, one widgeon, one pheasant, and two squirrels.

While I was stationed at Peking I kept my guns well oiled. Occasionally I went by train to Huailai for the shooting, and made a few good bags of duck, geese, and hare. I found it a good plan to take cover behind a peasant ploughing with a mule and a donkey, as the geese take no notice of ordinary field labourers. Then, by asking the ploughman to approach gradually towards the geese which were feeding in the fields, I was able to reach them with a right and left shot as they rose ponderously into the air.

Huailai is a small walled city on a sandy plain to the north of Peking. Here the Emperor Kwang Hsü and the Empress Dowager took refuge on their flight from Peking after the raising of the siege and relief of the Legations.

There is a cliff on the banks of a stream near by, which makes an excellent stance for flighting ducks. On the top was a small wayside shrine, just large enough to accommodate a camp bed at the foot of the altar, which bore an astonishingly ugly idol, over which hung a wooden tablet with the characters '*Chu Wei Chih Shen*', or God of Swine! Not being at all particular, I slept there occasionally, in order to be on the spot at the time of the early-morning flight.

One day I was stalking geese on one side of the river, and there was another sportsman on the opposite bank. I fired at the geese, bagged one, and the rest of the flock flew over the water, where they came within range of the other gunner, who immediately fired—and fell flat on his back as if he was hurt. I forded the stream as quickly as possible, and found him unconscious, his face blackened with gunpowder. His gun had burst at the breech, and the two barrels had split apart. I sprinkled him with water and he recovered, none the worse. He told me he had been using cartridges filled with a very high explosive, in order to get longer carrying power, and this was evidently too strong for the gun. It was a lucky escape. He had, certainly, an enormous bag of water-fowl, but he might easily have blown himself up as well as the gun!

The most useful gun for China is a 12-bore, and Nos. 2, 6 and 9 cartridges. The average gun will require about one thousand cartridges a year, depending on the amount of time he is able to give to the sport. A rifle is useful for bigger game, such as tiger, deer, and boar. Tiger-shooting is dangerous work, but chiefly on account of the fact that it is necessary to go far into the mountains, where brigands abound in the various caves and natural hiding-places, and do not hesitate to ambush the unwary traveller and kill him on the spot for fear of denunciation.

The farmers are delighted when tigers or wild boar are shot. The latter has his den in the wooded hills, whence he sallies forth to commit depredations on the crops below; sometimes the natives are able to snare them in deep pits dug at the foot of the mountains, and covered with fresh grass. Specimens over four hundred lb in weight, with ten-inch tusks, have sometimes been secured by the fortunate hunter. I have heard of tigers being killed by means of an explosive bait—a kind of land-mine attached to a piece of meat. Wild geese, etc., are sometimes caught with a bean-pod containing a bamboo spring, which uncurls in the bird's throat and chokes it to death!

Sporting-dogs are not bred in China to any great extent. The modern Chinese sportsman uses a small terrier. I should think a good pointing and retrieving animal could be produced by crossing the hunting-greyhound of Mongolia with good sporting foreign strains. This greyhound is probably the oldest pure breed of dog and, incidentally, Manchuria is believed to be the original stamping-ground of the small five-toed horse, from which all others were derived.

The ring-necked pheasant, *Phasianus torquatus*, is found in all parts of the country, and is easily distinguished by its broad white collar, as well as by the pale greyish-blue of its upper wing-coverts and rump. This bird has been introduced into English preserves, where it interbreeds readily with other species.

When I was in Hong Kong I often used to hear a bird whose cry seemed to resemble the invitation, 'Come to the peak, ha, ha!' This was the grey partridge, *Francolinus p. pintadeanus*, which finds a very comfortable sanctuary on the island, where shooting is not allowed.

When full grown it is about the size of a bantam hen, and it is speckled and barred with white and grey on a dark ground, partially tinged with russet.

I do not very much like killing snakes. I have always had a horror of them ever since a large cobra tried to finish me off in the bathroom in India when I was a small boy. However, I have often shot them in self-defence. The first I bagged disintegrated into small pieces, each of which wriggled off in a different direction. I often used to shoot them in my garden at Lungchow, which contained the dangerous bamboo snake, *Trimerisurus gramineus albolabris*, which has two pale yellow lines along each side of its grass-green body, and a reddish line on the tail; the head is triangular, like a viper's, and covered with small scales. A good thing to remember is that non-poisonous snakes usually have oval heads.

The terrible hamadryad cobra, which runs to fifteen feet, also occurs in the warmer districts, and is liable to attack on sight instead of trying to escape, as is the case with most other snakes. I saw two men walking along in Lungchow city one day carrying a large python tied to a pole. On inquiry I found it was to be sold in the market as food.

An animal fancier in Lungchow had a Siamese cat, which was noted for killing snakes. It was always on the look-out for them in the gardens and along the hedges at the side of the road. One day I happened to see this cat in action against a small viper. She seemed to realize that she had to keep out of range of the head when it struck at her. She was extremely cautious and very active, like a mongoose. Now and then her paw shot out with claws extended, and soon the serpent was bleeding in different parts of its body, and finally it lay without further movement. I examined it and its spine appeared to be broken in several places. I offered to buy this cat, but the owner refused to part with her. She would certainly have been very useful in my garden.

I cannot do better than close this record of sporting days in China with the following tiger story contributed by Mr G. W. Pearson, H.M. Consul, to *The Outburst*, a local periodical which I edited and produced at Ningpo in 1913. I can vouch for its veracity, because I was personally acquainted with the sportsmen in question, including Mr A., who, curiously enough, was later my chief in Hong Kong, and who told me that he was quite sure the mouse feels nothing when in the clutches of the cat, being paralysed, as *he* was when a tiger pounced upon him in the jungle and mauled him very severely!

TIGER-SHOOTING EXTRAORDINARY

Having had the privilege of reading about certain episodes of local gunnery, and as at present there is in the port a sportsman who is able to verify my statements, which might otherwise be doubted, it would appear an auspicious moment to relate some reminiscences of a year's shooting of big game in one of the remoter treaty ports.

On arrival thereat, life seemed somehow dull. Perhaps a steamer visited it weekly, perhaps not. The telegraphic communication was wanting. The community was sleepy (with the exception of the sportsman in question), so the advent of a typhoon was welcomed, even if, as was sometimes the case, the walls of all the compounds were laid low at one fell swoop, even though the mosquito-house was carried from our roof to a neighbouring garden some quarter of a mile away, and tigers, driven from the jungle by the falling trees, sought shelter in hospital, Customs and Consular compounds.

On two successive mornings after these typhoons, I was aroused from my beauty slumbers by callers; in the first instance a missionary lady rode in and asked my assistance in eliminating a tiger which had suddenly made its appearance for board and shelter during the previous night within her compound. She had escaped, somewhat dishevelled, through a back window, and came to me for advice and assistance.

Armed with a walking-stick and a substantial breakfast, and assured by the statement that the tiger was securely confined between four solid garden walls, I left my mosquito-netting blowing about and walked over the few hundred yards intervening to find *bona fide* tiger tracks galore, but no tiger.

On the second morning a dead tiger was brought to me, speared through by sharpened bamboos, and killed close to the Concession. This spurred me to take the matter up in earnest.

Armed with a Mauser automatic repeater and the office Martini-Henry, with a friend who shall hereafter be named A., my very delightful and plucky shooting companion in the adventures to be narrated, we visited the village of Yi Ma, some four miles from the Custom House.

Proceeding slowly and carefully over the plain, we came upon several mangled corpses, some half eaten, some merely rags and bones—the prey of the man-eaters! On the way we met several carts drawn by bullocks. In each were two life-size straw dummies, with false queues, one placed on each side of the live driver, and dressed in Chinese blue clothes. We inquired the reason, and were told that the tiger would spring from the jungle and seize the nearest figure, edible or otherwise. The dummies were apparently attached to every cart, but quite frequently the tiger would carry off the leading cow or buffalo from the team in preference to the vegetarian diet of pure straw and Chinese blue cloth!

Our first adventure was to come that night. Having assured ourselves fully on the evidence of innumerable tiger tracks and portions of dummies, etc., that there were at least six tigers of various sizes in the immediate patch of jungle, we tethered our ponies in a temple, removed our saddles, and took them, with a length of rope, to a majestic camphor tree in the centre of the jungle, with a pig which was calculated to squeal all night.

We tied up the pig to a stake, giving it a run of six yards of stiff new Chinese rope, and bestrode the saddles up in the branches of the tree.

Owing to mosquitos, cramp, prickly heat, thirst and excitement, there was no possibility of sleep, and when, at about ten o'clock, Mr Stripes hove his ten feet of body into view in the moonlight some three hundred yards away, even the faintest possibility vanished. So did he. We nearly did, too.

We waited until midnight, and, when the moonlight began to sink behind the trees, and shooting would soon become impossible, we drew lots as to who should descend, and stir up piggy, so that his plaintive, musical voice should be issued to Mr Tiger. A. lost and descended with speed, for there were no low branches to the tree. He goaded that poor pig around until the ground quaked, and the heavens awoke with squeals.

Suddenly, from out of the jungle, stole a dim, black shadow, creeping silently forward. It was the tiger! A. could not see it from his position on the ground. I was above, but could not fire to wound effectively. Slowly and relentlessly came the long, black, destroying shape. I called to A. He could not find the rope to the branch on which he had kept vigil, and was unable to find other shelter.

The only course I could think of as practical was to fire the Mauser automatic into the air as fast as possible in the hope of scaring the great brute before it could attack A., who was practically defenceless in the dark; but on it came; with one wrench the strong rope was snapped—and into the impenetrable forest quickly disappeared this big cat, together with the poor musical pig, whose bones we found—picked as clean as a whistle—on the following day.

Early next morning we set out to track down the majestic animal, which had been so oblivious of the danger of modern firearms, but found only recent tracks of a male, his mate, and two cubs, which had left the jungle for the neighbouring village.

The villagers told us to wait until four p.m., when the animals would return. We waited with rifles sighted at one hundred yards. The four tigers appeared over the crest of the sand-dune. Father tiger carried a large, heavy pig. Mother tiger a slightly smaller pig, and the cubs, piglets. Each looking well satisfied, all were in Indian file, trotting over the exact tracks they had made in the morning.

Father tiger disappeared into the jungle before we could get a clear sight at him. I broke the near foreleg of Mother tiger with the only shot which was fired. She did not, however, drop her pig until she got over the ten yards of sand into cover which obscured her from our view, but she left it almost immediately after, as we found it on tracking after her.

Next day came the dramatic climax, for almost at dawn I received an urgent message from A., saying the Father tiger was cornered. Without breakfast I mounted my pony and was with A. within the hour. A long morning's hunt followed, with the knowledge that *Felis tigris* was only about twenty yards ahead of us all the time.

A loud roar, and our carriers and beaters were up the trees like so many crows! At last we drove him to a small patch of jungle. I climbed a tree in order to try to locate him, but the underbrush was so thick that I could not see any sign of life—until up came Father tiger and sat down at my feet!

Owing to the dense cover I could only see about one square inch of the brute, panting and driven as he was, wounded and harried beyond measure. Still, there was the square inch, and luckily I had my rifle. I threw down cartridges, handkerchiefs, even dollars, but the great beast was too spent to rise and give me the chance of a vital shot, so I took deliberate aim at the target afforded—only twelve feet away—and fired. The animal sprang up, turned a complete somersault, and fell dead in the thick jungle.

Knowing (or perhaps not) how many tigers were in the district, we made up our minds to give it a rest until we had fortified the inner man. We went away and consumed our beer and sandwiches, shaking hands with each other, and incidentally, sitting unbeknown within a few feet of Mother tiger, who was lying wounded in a clump of bushes!

An hour later A. and I resumed our hunting. Needless to say, the natives had disappeared for good and all. A. entered the jungle from one side, I from the other, but after some time I went round to A.'s side to see if he had found the dead tiger, and followed up his track through the undergrowth. Suddenly he came reeling out into the open, more dead than alive, and bleeding from head to foot. He had been bitten in thirteen places by a further and unwounded tigress, the existence of which we had not even suspected!

The net result was this:

One European—badly hurt.

One European—bad touch of sun.

One tiger (male)—dead.

One tigress—wounded and lost.

One tigress—unwounded.

250 peasants—freed from marauding tigers.

CHAPTER 19

Hook, Line and Sinker

From the days of remote antiquity the art of fishing has been assiduously practised by the Chinese people, not only in most of the ways employed in other parts of the world, but also by a number of highly ingenious methods of their own invention.

Fishing as a recreation is chiefly enjoyed by the elderly Chinese gentleman who has retired to live in the country. When he wishes to ponder on some philosophical or literary matter, he leaves his hook unbaited so that the fish will not disturb his train of thought. He likes to absorb the atmosphere of his rural surroundings and feel at peace with Nature, and even if he is not a Buddhist at heart he will seldom take fish for pleasure.

Izaak Walton would, no doubt, have been interested in the psychology of the Chinese hermit who fishes happily without bait, and catches nothing but stray ideas. In my own case I always fish with bait, and have caught very little except old boots, so I can never lay claim to being classed as a 'compleat angler'. Nevertheless I take an admiring point of view of others who not only catch fish with bait but also without any bait at all!

China is well supplied with rivers, lakes, and canals, which contain innumerable species of fish, which are taken all the year round, chiefly with nets and bamboo traps, though rods and hand-lines are also employed to some extent. Many good eating fish go up the rivers to spawn, and their eggs are collected and reared in stew-ponds and wooden tubs.

The *Sam-lai* (a kind of sturgeon), carp, tench, and perch are all popular. The 'belt-fish' is caught on a hook with a wire trace baited with portions of fish, it is shaped like a long strap, and is most voracious, several being often taken on one hook, sometimes one fish holding on to the tail of another!

Trout are usually netted as they leap up the waterfalls to the higher levels. Young eels are often scooped up in hand-nets at the edge of the canals, but care has to be taken to avoid snakes, which are often indistinguishable from the eels.

I was particularly interested in an extraordinary batrachian which I caught in the West River. The Chinese call it *Kou-yü*, or dog-fish, and indeed it looks very much like a small dachshund! It has a smooth, black body about two feet long, four webbed paws, a flat tail, and a head resembling that of a dog. Its flesh is firm and tastes like lobster. This amphibious animal is also found in Mexico, where it is called *Axolotl*, or mud-puppy, and is really the undeveloped larva of the salamander known to science as *Amblystoma tigrinum*.

It undergoes a transformation of 'neotony' (Greek: *neosteino*, extend or stretch). This process only occurs if the water dries up or becomes scarce, in which eventuality the creature's gill-clefts close, the long fin of the back and tail disappear, and it leaves the dry river bed or lake bottom and becomes a lung-breathing salamander. The common newt has similar characteristics, being only aquatic during the spawning season, but the mud-puppy will breed and produce eggs either in the larval or fully adult salamander state; the larva is black, but when it changes to a salamander it acquires a variegated protective colouration. It is entirely unique for an animal to reproduce its kind before it reaches its complete adult state. It depends on the available supply of water. Whether the eggs are produced in the larval or fully developed stage, they hatch, nevertheless, into axolotls.

Perhaps I have had rather more success in sea-fishing than in fresh water, and I have caught bass and bream when on holiday. In Weihaiwei the bass are taken with rod and line baited with a rubber artificial frog. I have taken them with a celluloid prawn. In the Hong Kong waters I once caught a 'cow-fish', which actually has horns like a cow, though, fortunately, it is by no means the same size as that animal! It is covered in a coat of armour, in the form of a number of bony plates, so it may be regarded as a good friend but a bad enemy!

I was fishing with buffalo-meat one evening from the deck of a Customs cruiser anchored off the island of Samun in South China, when I felt a series of strong jerks on the line. With some difficulty I drew up a peculiar yellow crab with red spots, to which a fearsome-looking octopus was firmly attached. It was a terrible job disentangling this family party from the line. Old man octopus was happily engaged in sucking the juices from the crab, in which he had punched a neat hole with his hard beak. I returned the crab to the sea as it was probably poisoned by the salivary venom of the octopus, but I put the octopus into a bucket of water and went on fishing. After catching a vicious-looking eel with some trouble, I happened to look round and I saw Mr Octopus in the act of crawling down the gangway. I am perfectly convinced that he winked at me with his evil eye as he left the ship!

I was very fortunate in being able to make a close study of the Ningpo fisheries in 1913, when I wrote the following account of them, which appeared in the March number of *The Outburst*. This account was used as a Trade Report by the British Consul, printed in a British Government Blue Book presented to Parliament by command of His Majesty the King, and reprinted in the *Westminster Gazette*, the *New China Review*, and other publications.

THE NINGPO FISHERIES

Ningpo is the greatest market in China for fish of every kind, which is exported to nearly all native ports, and even to foreign countries.

The number of craft fitted out for the sea fisheries is over ten thousand in the Chusan archipelago. A licence must be procured for each boat from the civil authority. For fishing on the shores of the islands, application for space must be made to the officials, as the ground belongs to the Government. There are also special regulations for fishing in the lakes, rivers and canals. On payment of a small sum, a certain amount of space is granted by the officials, and a licence issued, but the holder is thenceforward held responsible for the preservation of the fish in his allotment. In order to keep the stock in good condition, a proportionate quantity of young fry must yearly be placed in the water, and no fishing is allowed during the spawning season.

Nets are manufactured at Taichow, one hundred and forty miles south of Ningpo, also at Chinhai, and in some of the small villages in the neighbourhood. Most of the nets are made of hemp twine obtained from China grass—*Urtica nivea*—tanned in a solution of mangrove bark and dipped in pigs' blood. Silk nets are made at Shaohsing. Fishing-lines are made of jute, hemp, coir, and silk; coarse ropes of twisted bamboo, straw, and reeds. Many kinds of fish traps are made of plaited bamboo.

As the chief fishing-grounds are at some distance from Ningpo, special ice-boats follow the fishing-junks to buy the catch and bring it back to Ningpo between layers of ice. Among the first objects which strike the eye on the approach to Ningpo from the seaward are the thatched, tent-like constructions in which ice is preserved during the summer. The bottom of these ice-houses is nearly on a level with the surrounding fields, and is generally about twenty yards long by fourteen broad. The walls, which are built of mud and stone, are very thick, twelve feet in height, and are in fact a kind of embankment rather than walls, having a door on one side level with the floor for the removal of the ice, and a sloping terrace on the other side, from which the ice can be thrown into the house. On the top of the walls or embankment a tall span roof is raised, constructed of bamboo, thickly thatched with straw, and in appearance exactly like a hay-stack. The Chinese, with characteristic ingenuity, manages to fill his ice-houses in a most simple way, and at a very trifling expense. Around the house he has a small level field connected with the river, from which he takes care to flood it before the approach of winter. The water thus freezes and furnishes the necessary supply of ice at the very door. Again in spring these same fields are ploughed up and planted with rice. The ice thus stored is used for preserving fish which are caught in vast quantities off the mouth of the river and in the Chusan archipelago.

Soon after the middle of March, the fleets set sail for the first season of fishing, the captains having selected by the almanac an auspicious day for so important a move, and paid due heed to their traditional maxims for prognosticating fine weather. This first fishing-season lasts about three months; the second, or winter season, is shorter.

Four kinds of craft are employed for the sea fisheries, viz:

(1) The *Pu ch'uan*, or 'catching ships', which take all sorts of fish with nets and lines.

(2) The *Ta-tui ch'uan*, or 'great pair boats', so named because they always go in pairs dragging a large net between them.

(3) The *Hsiao-tui ch'uan*, or 'small pair boats', a smaller kind of *ta-tui*.

(4) The *Wu-tsei ch'uan*, or 'black robber (cuttle-fish) boats', which are of small tonnage, and take cuttle-fish with nets.

Many varieties of fish are caught at sea—sharks, bass, mackerel, pomfret (*Stromateus argenteus*), rock cod, mullet, bream, conger, shad, etc., but of all kinds the most important, by far, is the cuttle-fish, of which Ningpo alone receives 40,000 to 120,000 *piculs* in good years, and the market price is increasing yearly, showing that the supply is not enough for the demand. Besides the ordinary method of taking cuttle-fish with nets, during the mating season a female cuttle-fish is sometimes towed on a line behind a boat; numerous males are attracted to her, and are then picked up in hand-nets.

Jelly-fish are used as food and caught with nets, and, nearer the shore, long conical nets, so disposed that they always present their aperture to the tide, are used for catching shrimps. Prawns and crabs abound in the sea, lakes, rivers, and canals, and oysters are cultivated at the head of Nimrod Sound. Cockles and mussels are also gathered on the rocky islets outside the Chusan group. A kind of solenoid (screw-shaped) shell, called by the natives *Ch'ing tzu*, and another mollusc known as *Ni lo*, or 'mud screw', are collected at low water and held in high esteem by Chinese gourmets.

On the mud flats, left along the coast by the receding tides, long nets are fixed vertically on bamboos, in the shape of a half-circle or of a labyrinth. Fish are left prisoners in these enclosures at low tide. A special kind of mud sledge is used by the natives to visit these weirs. The sledges, called *Ni ma*, or 'mud horses', are made of three small boards, and look like a long slipper or snow-shoe; they are five or six feet long and one foot broad. The structure is made solid by three cross-bars. In the middle two uprights, eighteen inches high, support a transverse bar. The fisherman, placing one knee in the middle of the sledge, and supporting himself by both hands on the bar, propels himself rapidly along over the mud by pushing with the other leg. Upon the sledge he carries a basket or two to hold his catch.

Many are the ways used in the Ningpo district for catching fish in the rivers, lakes, and canals, but none of them are more curious than the fishing with trained cormorants. The best cormorants come from Fenghua, Shaohsing and Tanghsichen. The birds sit along a rail in a small boat, and are urged into the water with a pole. Each cormorant has a ring or cord round its neck to prevent its swallowing the fish it catches, and its legs are connected by a short piece of string forming a loop by which refractory birds may at any moment be brought on board *nolens volens* with a long bamboo hook.

Another remarkable method of fishing is to be seen on the Ningpo River, called 'mirror fishing'. It is the catching of fish by moonlight, with a long, narrow, flat boat, provided on one side with a board sloping down into the water and painted a bright white. On the other side of this craft is a net stretched vertically on stanchions. The fish, attracted by the white board, jump on it, and thence into the boat—the net preventing them from falling into the water on the other side!

The natives also fish with the *Kan tseng*, or net and clapper. The net is spread on a light bamboo frame in the shape of a truncated pyramid. The fisherman either sits in a boat or wades in the shallows, striking the water with a wooden clapper which frightens the fish into the net. Sometimes this process is assisted by a man who sits in another boat and beats the bottom boards with a bundle of jangling iron rods.

The fish called *Lien yü*, a species of tench used as an offering to the gods by persons desiring the happiness of having children, is reared in reservoirs, while the *Li yü*, or carp, is to be found in ornamental fish-ponds in the temple grounds, etc., together with numerous beautiful varieties of goldfish of many different shapes and colours.

CHAPTER 20

Music and Drama

Music and Drama are very closely connected in China. In most cases the one is incomplete without the other, because orchestral and vocal music does not exist alone in the country to any great extent. There is no counterpart of the Albert Hall. The stage plays are interspersed with poetry or blank verse, which is sung for the most part in a high-pitched recitative, accompanied by the music of gong, flute, violin, etc. The gong is chiefly used to accentuate the highly dramatic phases of the action.

About the only occasion when music is heard alone is during the hymn of praise, which is sung and played during the biennial worship of Confucius. The Chinese also have a national anthem. There are also young girls who are trained to sing and play musical instruments at banquets.

Chinese music, in its pure and unadulterated form, originally entailed the study of the Five Elements: metal, wood, water, fire, and earth. It is governed by the Laws of the Universe, which lay down that there are Six Adverse Occasions when certain instruments should not be played, i.e. during intense cold; great heat; high wind; heavy rain; loud thunder; and a snowstorm. There are also Seven Unfavourable Conditions, namely within sound of mourning; or of other music; when occupied with prosaic affairs; if the body has not recently been bathed or the clothing is unclean; without burning incense; and in the absence of an intelligent listener.

Thus it is clear that music was a highly cultured art with a complicated symbolism. I should like to have taken part in it, even if only in the role of an 'intelligent listener'. Its calm, cool accents would compare, it seems to me, rather favourably with the disturbing effect of much of the ultra-modern music.

I made a collection of Chinese musical instruments in my bachelor days, but, unfortunately, after a rather merry party in the Mess on

New Year's Eve, they were seized and played so enthusiastically by my guests that they became somewhat disintegrated, and, on 'the morning after the night before', the house-coolie gathered up the *disjecta membra* and consigned them to the dustbin!

A friend of mine was an enthusiastic collector of antique musical instruments of all nations, and had about two hundred, which he hung up on the walls of his billiard-room. When I played billiards with him I sometimes played tunes as well, because the butt of my cue was apt to strike an African drum or an Egyptian harp, etc., on the wall behind me! I added a few Chinese instruments to his collection, which he bequeathed to the British nation when he died. A combined flute and sword-stick was a unique item, and must have been useful for purposes of self-defence when the gay serenader was challenged by a rival for the lady's affections!

It might be assumed that the Chinese Customs Service would not appear to be concerned with the music and drama of China or any other country, but nevertheless Sir Robert Hart employed a Chinese band to play in the Inspectorate gardens, where al fresco theatrical entertainments were also given occasionally by members of the staff, and by Chinese actors, jugglers and conjurers. Sir Robert also sponsored the publication, by the Customs Statistical Department, of an illustrated work on Chinese music, including the ritual worship of Confucius, prepared by Mr J. A. van Aalst, Commissioner of Customs. Concerts were also held quite frequently in the Shanghai Customs Club and elsewhere, at which individual members of the Service demonstrated their musical ability. We could produce many fine singers and instrumentalists.

At Shanghai I served, in 1906, with Mr Luigi de Luca, an Italian Deputy Commissioner in charge of the General Office, who was an artist to his finger-tips. Not only was he a contributor of a number of clever caricatures of local residents and members of the Customs (including myself) to the *Eastern Sketch*, but he also composed a very tuneful ballet entitled *Pierrot's Dream*. When I was appointed to the Peking Inspectorate, in 1919, I found Mr de Luca was the Staff Secretary there, and he produced his ballet at the local theatre, with the wife of a Chinese official as chief ballerina and several of the wives of members of the Customs staff as ladies of the ballet.

Mr K. Jordan, a Dane on the Inspectorate Staff, was also a fine musician, and he trained and conducted a band of various nationalities, including Chinese, who performed at Peking.

My wife and I, together with other Customs people, also took part in private theatricals in the British Legation Theatre and elsewhere. I have even ventured to sing in Chinese!

One of the favourite amusements of the people is going to the theatre. It has been said that every Chinese is a polished actor. Their daily life, with its ceremonial politeness, demands the constant exercise of histrionic talent. The passion for dignity, pomp, and show is so dominant in the national character that it is not astonishing to note the great popularity of the drama. Moreover, the bulk of the people are poor, and the luxurious embroidered costumes and scenes of great splendour to be witnessed, at small expense, in the theatre, serve to satisfy, to some extent, the general desire for a more sumptuous and colourful existence.

The most striking feature I noticed was the Shakespearian absence of properties, and the fact that actors, musicians, and theatre attendants occupied the stage together, but the theatres at the larger towns are now beginning to show the influence of the foreign drama by the introduction of curtains, wings, and scenery. The revolving stage has been in use for many years. The ceremonial dances are very spectacular, and the agility of the acrobats is most remarkable.

The external part of a Chinese play is indicated by signs and make-believe, by a few simple devices, and by the movements and dresses of the actors themselves. They are all fixed rigidly by convention and therefore well known to every Chinese playgoer. But they are not so apparent to the uninitiated, so a few of them are given below, as classified by Arlington and Lewisohn in their joint publication, *In Search of Old Peking*, 1935, pp. 275–7:

SYMBOLIC

Two tables, one on top of the other, covered with red cloth, and with a chair on top, indicate a throne or a judgement seat.

Two bamboo poles, with some calico attached, represent a city wall or gate.

A boat is generally represented by an old man and a girl with an oar, who move at a fixed distance from each other.

A snowstorm is represented by a man carrying a red umbrella, from the folds of which he shakes out a shower of white slips of paper.

A chariot is indicated by two yellow flags, with a wheel drawn on each, one held in each hand.

A whip held in the left hand shows that the actor is dismounting from, in his right hand is mounting, his steed.

ACTOR'S MOVEMENTS

Lifting his foot high up, he indicates he is stepping over the threshhold of a door.

Bringing his hands slowly together then closes the door.

A fan held close up to the face shows that he is walking bareheaded in the sun.

Walking slowly round the stage with both hands extended and feeling to both sides indicates walking in the dark.

Slowly moving the hands across the eyes denotes weeping.

Standing stiffly behind a pillar, he is in hiding.

Lifting the skirts, bending down at the waist, and walking with slow, measured steps, indicates the ascent of a ladder or stairs, or crossing a narrow plank on to a boat.

COLOUR AND DRESS

A red-painted face indicates a sacred, loyal personage, or a great Emperor.

A black face—an honest, but uncouth fellow.

A white face—a treacherous, cunning, but dignified person.

A white patch on the nose—a villain.

Devils have green, gods and goddesses gold or yellow faces.

An Emperor's robe is always yellow, embroidered with coiled dragons winding up and down.

High officials also wear yellow, but have dragons flying downwards.

A warrior's hat is bedecked with two long peacock's feathers.

A beggar is indicated by a silk robe with gaudy patches.

A gay woman is covered with jewellery and gaudy silk and satins.

A virtuous one is always clad in a plain, black gown with light blue trimmings on the sleeves.

A ghost is represented by an actor with a black cloth over head and face, or with a slip of white paper stuck on the cheek, or with a curl of white paper suspended from the head.

Death is indicated by a red cloth thrown over the face.

Two men carrying black flags show that evil spirits are roaming about looking for victims.

SOUNDS

Blowing of trumpets offstage heralds the approach of cavalry.

Fireworks indicate the appearance of a demon.

Two or three blasts of the trumpet indicate an execution taking place offstage.

I often went to the theatre in Shanghai and Peking. The best Chinese theatre in Peking was the Kai Ming Theatre near the main gate of the Tartar city. The most celebrated actor of the day was Mei Lan-fang, to whom I was introduced at Peking, and whom I saw later on acting in a command performance held in the Presidential Mansion at Peking in 1920, in a historical play of which a synopsis follows:

GENERAL YANG'S VISIT TO HIS MOTHER

In the time of the Sung dynasty General Yang Yen-hui was captured by enemies in the north. Being a handsome man, he was made the husband of one of the Princesses. He spent fifteen years in the north and all communication was cut off from China.

Later on the Sung Emperor appointed Yang Yen-chao, brother of Yang Yen-hui, to attack the northern enemies. Madame Yang, their mother, being well versed in military affairs, accompanied her son to the war.

When this news reached Yang Yen-hui, he was anxious to visit his mother. He could not obtain a passport, so he was naturally unable to go through the barriers. As he could find no way to attain his object, he became sad, and his wife, the Princess, observing his state of mind, asked him the reason. General Yang was compelled to tell her the truth. He promised, under oath, that he would return after visiting his mother one evening.

The Princess then arranged to secure a passport, with which General Yang went through the barriers without hindrance, and saw his mother, brother, and other members of the family. As he had promised the Princess that he would return, he could not stay very long, and he hurried back to the north.

At that time, it became known that General Yang had made this secret journey with a stolen passport. Empress Hsiao, the mother of the Princess, desired to have him executed, but he was finally pardoned upon the Princess's entreaties.

Here is a full Chinese orchestra, as originally laid down by the Chinese classic *Book of Ceremonies*, translated by Legge, the famous sinologue:

STONE
(1) Sonorous Stone; (2) Stone Chime.

METAL
(1) Bell; (2) Gong; (3) Gong Chimes; (4) Cymbals; (5) Trumpet.

STRINGS
(1) Lute; (2) Psaltery; (3) Balloon Guitar; (4) Three-stringed Guitar; (5) Moon Guitar; (6) Four-stringed Violin; (7) Two-stringed Violin; (8) Harpsichord.

BAMBOO
(1) Pandean Pipes; (2) Ceremonial Flute; (3) Common Flute; (4) Small Flute; (5) Clarionet.

WOOD
(1) Sonorous Box; (2) Musical Tiger; (3) Castanets; (4) Wooden Fish.

SKIN
(1) Large Barrel-drum; (2) Small Barrel-drum; (3) Rattle-drum; (4) Flat Drum.

GOURD
(1) Reed Organ.

CLAY
(1) Ocarina.

The above instruments are not all used at the same time. Some are included in the theatrical performances of historical plays; others. such as the stone chimes, large drums, flutes, and trumpets, are employed only in the ritual and religious services. One or two are seldom, if ever, used in modern days.

Foreigners were not allowed to witness the ceremony of the worship of Confucius, at which the old ritual music was performed, but, nevertheless, I managed to see it in 1909, in company with that well-known Chinese scholar and writer the late Mr L. C. Arlington, who enlisted the aid of the American Consul at Nanking to arrange with the Chinese authorities for us to be admitted as a special favour.

We were smuggled in quietly and concealed behind a massive stone pillar in the courtyard of the large Confucian temple. It was a dark night in spring, and the scene was illuminated by huge iron braziers and coloured lanterns. All the principal Chinese mandarins of the district had assembled in full regalia to do honour to the noble and venerable sage. They advanced humbly nine steps along the stone-paved courtyard, and prostrated themselves and bowed nine times, repeating this process until they arrived at the 'Moon Terrace' before the main hall containing the tablet of Confucius.

Plaintive archaic melodies were rendered by a band of flutes, drums, and stone chimes, accompanied by a ceremonial posturing dance performed on the terrace by men in civil and military costumes. An ode to Confucius was then recited and burnt as a sacrifice, together with rolls of silk and laudatory scrolls. A whole ox, together with a sheep and a pig, lay dead in large brass trays on the altars before the shrine. The ritual was concluded with a hymn of praise to the Master, beginning 'Confucius, how great is Confucius', the last notes dying away just as the dawn broke, and the crimson rays of the rising sun spread slowly over the crowd of worshippers—a glorious finale to a beautiful pageant!

CHAPTER 21

The Inner Man

It is a common saying that 'What we eat, we are'. Thus the roast beef of old England may have been chiefly responsible in the past for the building up of our lads of the bulldog breed; porridge produces the lanky and canny Scot; potatoes go towards the make-up of the lively and vivacious Irish temperament. It is even possible that the excessive belligerency of the German race may have been largely due to over-indulgence in beer and blood sausages!

In the Celestial Kingdom the same rule probably applies, and to the variety of indigenous foods, and the heterogeneous collection of animal, vegetable, and mineral products in the Chinese pharmacopoeia, may be ascribed, to a great extent, the general characteristics of the people. For instance, those who live near the sea show a greater brain development on account of the abundance of fish. The dwellers inland are often thin and underdeveloped, but this may be partly due to famine, floods, and civil war. The northerner has a fairly good physique owing to his heavy consumption of starchy and fat-forming foods, which tend, however, to make him rather stolid and less intelligent than the southern coastal folk, who eat more rice and fish. In mid-China, where there is only fresh-water fish, but more vegetables, we have a somewhat highly strung and slightly undernourished individual. The haulers of junks through the rapids of the Upper Yangtze are also badly fed, but this may be due to their low purchasing power. They often find it necessary—as do the chair-bearers, rickshaw-coolies, and cargo-carriers—to eat or smoke opium as a stimulant to take them through the excessively hard work they have to perform.

Chinese food, properly prepared, is extremely delicious, and most satisfying. Moreover, it has a texture and variety of flavour which are quite unique. The Chinese are the most hospitable people in the world, and when they invite their friends to dinner they usually provide a banquet fit for a king! In most cases, dinner-parties are held in a restaurant, as the average householder generally considers his own limited resources quite inadequate to do full justice to his guests.

Here is the menu of the first Chinese dinner I ever had, and to which I was invited by the Customs Taotai, or Superintendent, at Hankow in 1903, in the Wan Fu Fan Tien, or Restaurant of Ten Thousand Joys:

Melon Seeds
Assorted Fruits
Ginko Nuts
Almond Tea
Samshu
Roast Duck and Bamboo Shoots
Soya Bean Sauce
Stewed Carp and Ginger
Birds' Nest Soup
Sharks' Fins
Rice

There are many culinary delicacies such as *Pa Pao Fan,* or 'Food containing Eight Precious Things', which is a kind of mixed stew; as also is *Ch'üan Chia Fu,* or 'Joy of the Whole Family', the latter being usually prepared in a pewter chafing-dish in the centre of the table. Each province has its special dishes, due to local conditions, habit, personal inclination, and sometimes for medical or superstitious reasons. Peking is noted for its ducks' tongue soup and chicken-skin pancakes, Canton for its dried and varnished poultry, Shaohsing for its wine, etc. In Ningpo, I found that a favourite food was very small live crabs; when the cover is removed from the bowl, the crabs come out and are caught with chopsticks, dipped into bean sauce, and eaten alive, shell and all. It is believed that those which run the fastest are the most nourishing!

Beef is not eaten much by Buddhists, who are, theoretically, vegetarians. Only very old cattle are killed for food, and then the meat is too tough to digest. The yellow cow is chiefly used for ploughing, as also is the water buffalo. Mutton is consumed chiefly by Mohammedans, who sometimes roast whole sheep in the open air on their festival days. Pork is generally reserved for high days and holidays.

The following amusing description of a Chinese feast was given by my late aunt, Miss F. M. Williams, in her book, *A New Thing*:

Several small tables were placed in different parts of the room; eight people sat at each, the men on one side of the room and the women on the other. We sat amongst the women. There were several little bowls on the table, filled with various kinds of food—little pieces of chicken stewed in gravy, with roasted chestnuts and vegetables, fat pork and gravy, prunes, figs and nuts. Each person had a bowl of rice, and chopsticks, and could fish out bits of chicken, or pork, and pop them into her neighbour's bowl or her own mouth, as she liked. One woman put some chicken into my bowl, and I was enjoying it very much, and getting on nicely with my chopsticks, when suddenly another woman put in a spoonful of pork fat and *three* spoonsful of pork gravy! It is against the rules of etiquette to refuse anything; so I was obliged to thank her. After a minute or two I put all my pork into my next-door neighbour's bowl, and so got rid of that. But the gravy I could not so easily dispose of; it had got mixed up with the rice, and it is *not* correct to give away your rice. I was obliged to give up eating any more, and finished up my dinner with figs and nuts! It is proper to throw all the bones, and anything you do not want, on the floor, so you can picture what the ground was like! But as the Chinese indulge in mud floors, and not in elegant carpets, it is not as bad as it *might* be!

Except on festive occasions, the average Chinese does not eat very much, as he is of a frugal disposition. No food is wasted, and children are taught to finish every grain of rice in their food-bowls. Very little is served cold, and the wine is also heated. I once tried to live exclusively on Chinese food for a month, but I must say I missed my usual ration of meat. In my opinion the Chinese should eat more meat. History shows that the dominating races of men have always been flesh-eaters.

The accepted method of communal feeding from the same central dishes is perhaps rather insanitary. Some Chinese agree that to put chopsticks into the mouth and then plunge them into food eaten by others may quite well convey the germs of infectious diseases. Rice is consumed in rather too large quantities, and would probably be more nourishing if mixed with barley. Peanuts and lotus-seeds are swallowed at all times, especially by children, whose stomachs are often seen to be unduly enlarged in consequence.

On the whole, the Chinese dietary is better than that of many
other countries, especially during periods of food rationing after war.
As a matter of fact, the scale of food in all countries is deserving of
more attention than is given at present, in order to produce a sound,
healthy people, capable of doing their work with the greatest possible
efficiency, both in their own interest, as well as in the interest of the
State concerned.

Dr John Abernethy (1764–1831), the celebrated Irish surgeon,
was the first Occidental specialist to prove that local diseases had a
constitutional origin from disorders of the digestive system, but Fu
Hsuan, a Chinese statesman of the Chin dynasty, said in A.D. 270:
'Disease enters in at the mouth and evil proceeds from it', i.e. due
caution should be observed in eating and speaking.

The Chinese often have recourse to stimulants such as opium,
ginseng, and deerhorns. Opium is the only real stimulant of these
three, and, taken as a medicinal tonic in reasonable doses, there
would be no harm in it, but unfortunately the people never know
where to draw the line, and they take too much and develop the drug
habit. The Government prohibits the use of opium, which checks the
abuse to some extent, but it is still grown in remote districts, and
smuggled throughout the country in considerable quantities.

Ginseng, or the dried root of the *Panax quinquifolia*, is believed to
possess magic potency for extension of life, etc., owing chiefly to its
fancied resemblance to the human form (cf. the ancient beliefs in the
power of the mandrake). It is a slight stimulant of little practical
value. The Chinese pay fabulous prices for 'old wild ginseng', but in
nine cases out of ten they are only buying the specially cultivated
root, trimmed and shaped and treated with hair ligatures to simulate
the rings of age.

The horns of the muntjac, antelope, and gorral are pulverized and
eaten as a cure for debility and senile decay, chiefly because the deer
is a conventional emblem of longevity. This material contains a small
percentage of ammonia, and is of no use at all—except as a faith cure.

Tigers' bone soup is consumed by robbers and bandits in the belief
that the strength and fierceness of the animal will pass into the
consumer. On the execution of a notorious pirate in Shanghai some
years ago the blood of his severed carotid artery was collected by the
bystanders, who drank it in the hope of acquiring boldness and
courage!

Bezoar, derived from the Iranian (Persian) *padzahr*, an antidote for poison, is a substance found in the stomach of the cow, goat, gazelle, bear, monkey, and snake. It merely consists of such extraneous matter as chalk, resin, hair, etc., which the animals have been unable to digest. The Chinese regard it as an excellent tonic, but it certainly must be most deleterious, and equally indigestible to human beings. The gall from the bladder of the ox, bear, and tiger is also consumed, because the gall-bladder is regarded as the seat of courage. Thus it will be seen that various products are taken internally, for nourishment of the body, for stimulation of the mind, and for materialistic, therapeutic, or symbolic reasons.

From very ancient times the Chinese have been interested in specifics, medicinal and magical, for the regeneration of the energies, and extension of the span of life. The Chinese pharmacopoeia contains a number of very strange substances, such as donkey-skin glue, which contains glycine, systine, lysine, argenine, and hystidine, and is said to improve the calcium nitrogen absorption of the body. There are also many vegetable preparations from the leaves of the dandelion, mulberry, nasturtium, shepherd's purse, amaranth, etc., as well as orange and pumelo peel, soap-plant thorns, verdigris, dried centipedes, etc., prescribed as remedies for various ailments. The eyes of certain animals, fish, and birds are also administered for different kinds of eye diseases, and hydrophobia is treated by application of the dog's brain to the wound!

Mushrooms are very delicious, but doctors are agreed that they have little food value. The Chinese think otherwise and regard them as highly nutritious and even conducive to long life. A species of rare fungus, possibly the *Polyporus lusidus*, is called by the Chinese *Ling chih*, or the Plant of Immortality. He who finds it is said to become immortal. Up to date only certain Taoist fairies have succeeded in locating it!

Many varieties of fungus are consumed, some grown on dead trees, others on mounds of earth. Some grow wild at the roots of trees or on rocks, some are credited with the power of casting out devils, others are said to cause irrepressible laughter!

There is an extraordinary combination of animal and fungus known as *Tung-ch'ung-hsia-ts'ao*, or 'winter worm summer grass'. This is a fungoid growth on a caterpillar, *Cordyceps chinensis*; the fungus grows from the animal's head as a parasite to the length of several inches, finally killing the caterpillar, which is then gathered, dried, tied in bundles, and sold in the market as a food and medicine!

I happened to be passing through the Lungchow city market one day, when I noticed a quack doctor, with a white beard and large eye-glasses, sitting behind a street stall on which were displayed a number of heterogeneous medicinal preparations and cure-all remedies, such as Tiger Balm for rheumatism, Deer Horn Essence for senile decay, Centipede Wine for colic, etc. There was also a clotted mass, which looked like a piece of horsehair stuffing from an arm-chair, and was labelled 'Dragons' Nest'. I found, on inquiry, that this material had been brought in from the country by a peasant who had discovered it in the distant mountains. It was guaranteed as an unfailing charm against battle, murder, and sudden death, if a small quantity were burnt and the ashes consumed in a cup of tea!

There are many other supposed products of the Dragon, which are used as charms and sovereign remedies for various ills of the flesh. A peculiar red gum is formed on the fruits of the rattan palm (*Calamus draco*) and is regarded by the Chinese as the veritable blood of the Dragon, and is used as a cure for ague. Ambergris is believed to be the dried saliva of the Dragon, and is also employed medicinally. The fossilized teeth of extinct animals are called Dragon's Teeth, and are pulverized and taken as a tonic; their bones are classed as Dragon's Bones, and used in a similar manner. Thus the Dragon, that age-old protector of China, dead or alive, exerts a powerful influence on the minds and bodies of many of the people.

It would be a good idea to institute in China, as in foreign countries (if it has not been done already), a General Medical Council, which would undertake the publication of a new and thoroughly revised Chinese Pharmacopoeia, in place of the so-called *Pen Ts'ao*, or Herbal, compiled in 1590. This measure would do much to counteract the purely superstitious remedies employed by the quack doctors of the old school, who still exist in some districts, and often do more harm than good. At the same time, some of the old Chinese drugs, which have proved efficacious, should be retained, and classified accordingly. The Chinese Government is fully alive to this necessity, and has already taken certain steps along these lines.

CHAPTER 22

Back to Nature

The Chinese is a true lover of Nature, and his greatest delight is to admire the beauties of the countryside. He is a born gardener and the country is practically nothing but one vast garden. Hence the term *Hua Kuo*, or Flowery Land, as applied to China, is certainly no misnomer. Almost every available inch of land is fully cultivated, and the Chinese are real experts in agricultural production.

The farmer is the backbone of the country. He works hard, and, as he enjoys it, he is always happy. 'To plough the earth and sing' is a quotation from Chinese poetry, and denotes the acme of felicity. Even the women make good 'land girls'.

An extraordinary devotion to flowers has prevailed from early ages among the Chinese. Many towns are provided with a public garden named after the first President of the Republic. A large number of beautiful flowers grow wild in the countryside. The Ningpo hills are ablaze with azaleas in the spring. Further south, more tropical flowers are seen in great profusion and a variety of colour, filling the air with fragrance.

The chrysanthemum and peony are the most popular bedding-out plants. Many garden varieties originated in China. The chrysanthemum, perhaps the most variable of all cultivated flowers, is derived from two wild species, and is mentioned in the ancient Chinese classics. We owe to the skill of the Chinese many kinds of roses, lilies, camellias and peonies; and from China have been introduced many of the most ornamental plants in our gardens, such as wisteria, diervilla, kerria, incarvillae, deutzia, primula, hemerocallis, etc. The peach and several varieties of orange are also natives of China.

The varnish tree (*Rhus vernicifera*) from which lacquer is obtained; the tallow tree (*Sapium sebiferum*); the white mulberry, on which silkworms are fed; and the tea plant, were all first utilized by the Chinese. A number of medicinal plants also originated in China, and of these ginseng and rhubarb are the best known. Nearly all our vegetables and cereals have their counterpart in China, where there are many varieties not yet introduced into Europe, though some, like the soya bean, are now attracting great attention.

A wealth of Chinese symbolism is based on the beauty and utility of the indigenous plants and trees, for every individual takes a great interest in the flora of the country.

The vegetable kingdom is more carefully studied and exploited for its food products than in any other country. Every day, women can be seen gathering herbs to be made into soups and salads, or concocted into medicines.

The lotus is highly popular, and it also has a religious significance. Buddha sat in contemplation on the margin of a lake, and rested his weary body. He compared the pure lotus buds rising from the black mud to virtue rising triumphant from a wicked world. The 'Jewel on the Lotus', i.e. the drops of water rolling about like crystal balls in the cup of the jade-green leaf, symbolizes the Buddhist truth.

The lakes in the old Imperial Forbidden City of Peking were the pride and joy of the various sovereigns of the former dynasties, especially in the early summer, when they were adorned with a wealth of rose and ivory lotus-buds amidst a profusion of verdant foliage.

Time marches on with relentless determination; Emperors pass away, Presidents arise, and, though the sun sets and the dew-drop sinks into the star-lit pool—as the weary Buddhist soul relapses into remainderless Nirvana—yet the glorious beauty of the lotus continues unfailing year after year, an emblem of hope for a brighter future.

In the near-by temple you may hear the priests at their daily orisons, chanting in deep reverberating tones, 'Om mani padme hum' (O the Jewel on the Lotus); and, in our imagination, we may see the Empress Dowager and the ladies of the Court, in her decorated barge, weaving in and out among the lotus blossoms in the cool of the evening.

The lotus festival is held in the summer, on a night when the moon is full, and the lotus lantern boats, made by placing a lighted candle on a lotus leaf, are set afloat and carried hither and thither by the wind and the stream with a most picturesque effect. Not only does this attractive flower provide food for the aesthetic senses but also for the physical needs, as the roots and seed-pods are eaten, while the leaves serve the grocer with convenient wrapping material for the dried fruits and other sundries which he purveys.

According to Chinese legend, a flower presides over each month of the year, and the 'Hua Chao', the birthday, or anniversary, of the flowers, is celebrated on the fifth day after the new moon. Flower shows are arranged on such floral days, when songs are sung and poetry is read in praise of particular flowers. In case other blossoms should feel neglected, there is a general anniversary of all flowers on the twelfth day of the second month, when it is customary to visit one's friends and present them with cuttings or little packets of seed.

I once heard of a Chinese beggar who had a sprig of jasmine growing in a broken pot. He guarded it from the cold winds with his tattered garments, and shared with it the contents of his meagre cup of tea. When it showed signs of drooping with the heat, he sat down and fanned it, and built a little paper shade over it to form shelter from the burning rays of the noonday sun. Finally it blossomed, and, as he regarded it, he forgot his poverty in the delight of its beauty and fragrance.

The chief agricultural products of the country are rice, maize, wheat, groundnuts, and soya beans. Most of the world's aniseed is produced in Kwangsi. Human labour is the main source of energy, and many of the farming instruments are as old as the country. The farmer worships the rain-bringing Dragon, the sun-producing Phoenix, and the gods of the land and the soil, whose shrines are often seen in the fields.

There are a certain number of cultivated trees, such as the cassia, wood-oil tree, camphor, and kapok. As so much of the brushwood is chopped out for firewood, the hills are denuded and storms have swept away the topsoil. Hence, after the annual rainy season every summer, large tracts of country are inundated, resulting in wholesale destruction of the crops, and general starvation of the people. If reafforestation were taken seriously, many of the barren hills could again be clothed in valuable forest timber.

China is well supplied with fruit. I have grown plantains and bananas at Kongmoon, raspberries at Wenchow, and lemons and peaches on the Indo-Chinese border. In Peking I grew good figs and grapes; the latter were coiled up and covered with earth in the winter. In my Lungchow garden was a tree which bore the so-called 'false mangoes', which the Chinese name 'Heavenly Peaches'. They are delicious, but if you eat more than two at a time you are liable to suffer from the most painful colic. There was also a fruit called the 'Miraculous Fruit'. After eating one, everything, even a lemon, tastes sweet. It creates this effect by temporarily paralysing the papillae of the tongue. The local jack-fruit, or 'Tree Pineapple', has a delightful flavour, but a very devastating smell—far worse than all the drains of the world. Pawpaws, pumeloes, pineapples, oranges and mango-steens are common in the south.

In Wenchow, Chekiang Province, I made a garden. It was a curious three-cornered shape and contained a hill on which was a Chinese grave. The Customs had bought the ground, but were unable to buy the grave, so, twice a year, the owner came with his family and worshipped his ancestor! I managed to buy for the Service an adjoining plot, which made the garden square, and I planted a small orchard of pomegranates, plums, oranges, and bananas. Flowers were larger and trees more luxurious than else-where. In fact, I erected a fence of fir-posts between the orchard and the tennis-court, and these posts immediately took root, put out leaves and grew into trees! Telegraph poles in the district occasionally behaved in the same way.

Our Wenchow house was covered with the most beautiful Gloire de Dijon roses, which, I was told, had been originally planted by Lady Hosie, the daughter of the late Rev. W. E. Soothill, the great sinologue and missionary, who once lived there.

I kept bees, not particularly on account of the honey, but because they double the fertility of the flowers and increase the production of the fruit by carrying pollen to the blossom, which might otherwise not all receive it. A very curious hybridization resulted from this intensive pollination. A cross between a coxcomb and a snapdragon was produced, and I always regretted I did not send it to Kew Gardens. The Wenchow coxcomb grows very large. It is red or yellow and spreads out into an enormous fan with crinkled edges. All along the rim of the hybrid 'fox-comb', which I called it, were innumerable antirrhinum blossoms, for all the world like a dainty fringe of coloured bells. The effect was most extraordinary, and also bore some resemblance to a festoon of Chinese lanterns! This reminds me of an invention of my Peking gardener, who was very fond of grafting chrysanthemums of different colours on a single plant—a wild variety growing on the old Tartar wall.

Many interesting varieties of bamboo grew in Wenchow, such as the tall temple bamboo, the dwarf 'heavenly bamboo', and the square bamboo—a speciality of that district. The bamboo groves flourished near the banks of the mountain streams and formed an elegant background to many a beautiful waterfall. They were also the favourite haunts of the woodcock and the pigeon.

My Lungchow garden was full of tropical vegetation of all the colours of the rainbow. There were palms, bamboos, flame-of-the-forest (*Poinciana regis*), wild roses, azaleas, hibiscus, camphor, and ginko. There were lemons, peaches, and pineapples. Croton, in many variegated and brilliant forms, added a highly decorative note. Each May, an enormous white gardenia came into full bloom just under the veranda.

The Chung Shan Kung Yuan, or Public Garden dedicated to the memory of Dr Sun Yat Sen, at Lungchow, is a peaceful place wherein to sit and meditate on a summer's evening. Bright-hued flowers are grouped together—dahlias, magnolias, and roses; in the lake, so artistically fashioned in the centre, are floating water-lilies and aquatic grasses. Dragon-flies of many kinds speed over the surface of the water in their continual search for edible insects, and sometimes they even attack each other.

Natural rocks have been adapted and formed into a grotto, in which sits a stone Buddha, with a benevolent smile on his countenance. There is a pavilion high-perched on a cliff overlooking the swift-flowing river. In it is a round table and seats of blue granite. On a large rock is carved in fancy characters the words, 'Do not forget the country's shame!' in reference to annexations of Chinese territory by outsiders in the past. Chinese children, half-naked, play shuttlecock with their feet, or feed the various birds and animals which are exhibited in wired-off enclosures. From the pavilion one may conveniently observe the surrounding mountains. These are of calcareous formation and are grouped in irregular chains. Many of the peaks are as much as one thousand five hundred feet high, but they average about six hundred feet.

When you walk in the garden during the hot weather you will not fail to hear the music of the cicada, or katy-did. The male sings throughout the summer to attract the female, the music emitted—much admired by the Chinese—being produced by the sibilant vibration of two flaps or *lamellae* situated in the thorax of the insect. The Oriental song-thrush will also be in evidence, with its loud and cheerful call, though there is a variety with a black head known as the laughing thrush, whose note is harsh and unmelodious. Blackbirds, flycatchers, shrikes, golden orioles, and kingfishers may be observed. Starlings and mynahs are often seen flocking together. The mynah follows the plough and perches on the backs of water-buffaloes; it talks as well as a parrot; its Chinese name is *Pa-ko*, meaning Eight Brethren, as it is said to fly in flocks of eight.

Sparrows are nesting under the tiles of the roofs and wage continual warfare with the crows and magpies, which eat their eggs. The bunting with its familiar 'tsic-tsic,' frequents the hedges and bushes, the yellow-breasted variety, known as the 'rice-bird' being netted in large numbers and sold for food. The swallow flies swiftly over the river in search of insects. Wagtails and pipits are seen in the marshes and grasslands, uttering their characteristic cries of 'chi chi chee chee chee'. The South China skylark is occasionally seen fluttering upwards with exultant song. The brown wren-warbler makes its nest in the bamboo groves, and has a peculiar call exactly like the mewing of a cat.

All these birds are plentiful in the gardens in the summer, but many of them seem to migrate to warmer regions in the winter, except a few such as the crow, magpie, jay, pheasant, etc. The collared crow, *Corvus torquatus*, has a white ring round the neck, and black plumage glossed with purple; it is chiefly found in the plains and valleys around the villages in the vicinity of water. The jackdaw, under parts white, and remainder black and purplish-blue, with white streaks on the head, is seen in chattering family parties. The magpie, black and white, and tail flecked with metallic green, is generally found in flocks near houses; it is much admired by the Chinese, who call it the Bird of Joy. The jay has a violet head and body, red beak, and long black and white tail; it is more common in the hills. The Hoopoe, *Upupa longirostris*, is the size of a thrush, has a golden-crested head, and black and white plumage. Various tits and nut-hatches are also regular visitors to the gardens.

It gives the Chinese gentleman great pleasure to take his cage of song-birds and hang it up on a tree in the park, but, curiously enough, the Government regards it as an effeminate habit, and has forbidden this simple pleasure. Nevertheless the Chinese will always appreciate the beauties of Nature so lavishly displayed around them in the beautiful Flowery Land.

CHAPTER 23

The Dragon's Lair

Of all the ancient Chinese beliefs, none is more interesting than that concerning the Oriental Dragon, who is by no means the gruesome monster of the medieval imagination, but the genius of strength and goodness. He is the guardian of the hills and streams, and presides over the destinies of the six hundred million inhabitants of China. He causes the winds to blow and produces rain for the benefit of the crops.

We can almost visualize him, surrounded by his nine children, so varied in their characteristics, playfully chasing each other in the waters of some sylvan stream; or, with his head of a camel, horns of a deer, eyes of a rabbit, ears of a cow, neck of a snake, belly of a frog, scales of a carp, claws of a hawk, and palm of a tiger, his lengthy and massive body stretched along the mountain gorges, lifting up his voice, which is as the beating together of innumerable copper pans, in the crashing of the mighty thunder!

Chinese legend has it that this scaly monster has selected Lungchow, *lit.*: 'Region of the Dragon', as his favourite resort. He is believed to be sleeping peacefully at the junction of three rivers which meet at this spot. His head and right paw are said to be sleeping peacefully in the Kaoping River, his left paw is stretched out in the Sungchikiang, and his body and tail lie along the Tsokiang. Thus he is the *Genius loci*, or presiding deity, of Lungchow, in the province of Kwangsi.

When I received instructions to proceed to this home of the Dragon, I recollected the Chinese saying:

> 'Who will beard the Dragon in his lair,
> Or take the cubs from a Tiger's den?'

and I accepted the challenge, because I feel that the good old Dragon, whose Occidental relative has figured on the armorial bearings of my native land of Wales since the twentieth century, is my *Deus ex machina*, and a general guide, philosopher, and friend in all my excursions. Thus I had the opportunity of actually residing in the very Lair of the Dragon, an old acquaintance, upon whom I relied to take under his temporary custody one more human being, who, though not of the celestial race, is, nevertheless, a strong partisan and sympathizer with the inhabitants of the Dragon's domain.

The journey to this remote outpost can be accomplished in several ways; by air and by boat, for instance, but the most convenient and practical is *via* Haiphong and up the Indo-China Railway to Langson near the Kwangsi border, where a motor car may be obtained for the final three hours run.

I arrived at Haiphong, from Hong Kong, by the Butterfield and Swire s.s. *Kwangtung*. Haiphong is the port of Tonkin, thirteen miles from the sea. It had 75,000 inhabitants, but I only saw a few; the rest were having their usual afternoon *siesta*, as it is too hot to work except in the morning.

I left by the evening train for Hanoi, sixty miles on, and spent the night there. Hanoi is noted for its wide-hatted flower girls, and its long months of humid heat. It is the capital of Indo-China (now Vietnam). The native streets were interesting and colourful, with their goldsmiths, potters, ivory-carvers, and lacquer-makers at work, while numerous silk merchants offered beautiful embroidered sarongs and tapestries for sale.

My personal relations with the local Annamites were rather unsatisfactory. While I was riding in a rickshaw my hat was snatched off my head by a ruffian who immediately disappeared up an alley! I bought another hat, but was careful to hold it on with both hands. At my hotel I was advised to lock my bedroom door in my absence, on account of thieves, as the hotel took no responsibility for losses incurred because of the activities of the light-fingered gentry of the neighbourhood. I locked the door and put the key in my pocket. When I went in again I noticed the hotel servant was making the bed, so I thanked him for his services and gave him a tip. I suppose he had a second key, which must have been very useful to him because, after I had gone I discovered that he had helped himself to a new flannel coat out of my suitcase!

Unfortunately, I had been given wrong information at Hong Kong, and I continued along the railway to Nacham, instead of Langson. Though I had telegraphed in advance from Hanoi for motor transport to the Nacham station-master, on my arrival there I found nothing had been done. This did nothing to improve my opinion of the Annamites! Finally, I discovered an old motor bus, had the seats removed, loaded the luggage on it, and engaged an ancient and hoary car, entirely devoid of springs, for myself.

There was a chauffeur and two assistants in my car, and a chauffeur and one assistant in the bus. They informed me that their vehicles were not licensed to leave Indo-China. As I was not prepared to take up permanent residence among the Annamites, whose character-istics I was beginning to dislike, I decided to apply for a permit from the French authorities.

After some difficulty, and many misdirections, I found the Com-mandant of the barracks. He was standing to attention, with his guard of Annamite soldiers smartly turned out in double ranks, with fixed bayonets. I felt very gratified with this reception, but I sub-sequently discovered that it was actually in honour of the Governor of Indo-China, who was about to arrive on a tour of inspection!

I handed my card to the Commandant and requested a permit for the cars. He said, however, that he had no power to issue such per-mits, and that I must apply at Dong-dang for it. So we proceeded ding-dong, and hell-for-leather, to go to Dong-dang!

At the Dong-dang frontier we were directed by the police to an Annamite official, clad in a very gorgeous uniform, who called for my passport, read it upside-down, and sent us on to the office of the Delegate on the top of a steep hill. The Delegate, a French officer, referred us to the Douanier, or Customs officer, for the necessary permit.

I now felt I was on more familiar ground, but on applying at the Custom House, I was informed by a young lady Annamite that the Douanier was in his bath. His ablutions over, after some time he put out his head, draped in a large bath-towel, over the upper veranda railing, and declared that he never issued such permits. We must apply to the Dèlegué, he said. I informed him in my best and most polite French that we had just come from the Dèlegué. 'Well,' he said, 'you had better go back to him again!'

By this time we were thoroughly soaked in perspiration, but, remembering that none goes so far as he who knows not where he is going, and that only when the way is unpleasant is the arrival fully assured—as the Indian philosopher has it—we climbed up the Hill of Despair once more in order to continue this vicious circumlocution!

I explained very carefully to the Delegate (who was most surprised to see us again) that we were entirely checkmated, and, under the excruciating circumstances over which we had absolutely no control, we most humbly solicited some official form of *laissez-passer* which might help to ease us through the forbidding and hostile barrier! Eventually he wrote down, at my dictation, what I considered to be a useful permit and safeguard against all let, hindrance, or barratry on our adventurous journey. I hope the office carbon copy of this document will serve as a useful guide for the printing of a suitable form for use in subsequent cases.

All was now well. The Delegate was quite affable and told me that I should have the honour of *doubling* the European population at Lungchow, as, previous to my arrival, M. Henri Bonnafous, the French Consul for Lungchow and Nanning, was the entire and unique foreign representative! I was deeply affected to think that I should bear the grave responsibility of figuring so largely in the Lungchow census records.

The cars now bumped their way, merrily but painfully, to Namkuan, or the 'Porte de Chine', the entrance to China—a gate of arched brick, surmounted by a watch-tower, and flanked by lofty walls running up the sides of the adjacent hills. These walls, which are six hundred feet long on either side, were built in imitation of the Great Wall of China.

Within the Gate, on Chinese soil once again, I breathed a sigh of relief, and was greeted at my own Customs Sub-Office with a fusillade of fire-crackers as a sign of welcome. The Chinese Dragon was evidently in a good mood.

After calling on the Chinese Frontier Delegate, Mr Huang Ting Hui, and obtaining further permits, while being attacked by hordes of voracious mosquitoes, we proceeded past various barriers along a narrow mountain road, and through wild and beautiful scenery consisting of deep ravines, jagged cliffs, tropical jungle, and rippling waterfalls. Above floated masses of smoke-grey, rose, and lemon-coloured clouds, gradually changing to flaming orange and vermilion as the sun set slowly behind the irregular horizon. The only illumination was provided by millions of fire flies,which escorted me into the town of Lungchow at the hour of 9.30 p.m. on the 24th April 1935, with the temperature at 85° Fahrenheit.

I found a Chinese dinner provided for me by the kindness of Mr Chen Shao, and very glad I was to have it. Seated in my new home, a brick bungalow, with a wooden veranda raised several feet off the ground, and standing in a garden of some size, terraced down to the river bank and thickly planted with tropical trees, I could not help wondering what was in store for me.

It was not long before I unpacked my bed-linen and retired to rest, just as the night-watchman began to beat his rounds on a bamboo drum as a sign of vigilance on behalf of the newcomer.

Thus I arrived, after six weeks' travel from London, at Lungchow, the 'Region of the Dragon'.

Lungchow was originally known as Lungpienhsien, or the 'District of the Dragon's Coils', the shorter name of Lungchow being used after the Han dynasty. It was opened to foreign trade, chiefly for political reasons, by Convention with France in 1887. It was to be a port of *liaison* between the French of Indo-China and the Chinese across the border.

In 1923 its population had risen to 25,000, but in 1930 the city was seized by Communists, and murder, incendiarism, and looting took place on a large scale, resulting in the desertion of the town by most of its inhabitants. In 1935 there would appear to be about 14,000.

It was on the 19th February 1930, that the Communist congress met at Lungchow, and decided to expel all foreign residents, and seize the French Consulate, Catholic Church, and Custom House. On the following day a band of 'Reds', headed by one Yu Tso Yu, entered and looted the French Consulate, and arrested the Consul and his wife. The mob then proceeded to the Custom House and Staff Quarters, which were likewise looted and interiors greatly damaged.

The Commissioner of Customs escaped through the garden along the bank of the river with two French priests, while the Chinese Staff went away in sampans and took refuge in a sand-bank. Later the Commissioner and the priests fell in with a Chinese bandit and his men, who offered to escort them to French territory for a small reward. Afterwards they demanded more, finally agreeing to a ransom of eight thousand dollars, which was duly paid at the frontier. On receipt of the money, however, the bandits foolishly discharged their guns at their erstwhile captives, without effect, but bringing upon themselves a withering fire from the French frontier guards, resulting in several casualties.

During the month of 'Red Terror', heavy contributions were

exacted from the local merchants. Numerous persons were executed by the Communists, who were eventually driven out of the city by the Provincial Government forces under Commander Liang Chao-chi a month later.

The Customs was first reopened at Namkuan, on the Tonkin frontier, on the 1st May 1930, with the Staff residing at Langson. Finally, after the suppression of various lawless bands of brigands in the district, and the restoration of peace and order, Customs work was resumed at Lungchow on the 9th March 1931, under a Chinese Commissioner, in a rented office. The original Custom House and Staff Quarters were reconditioned and occupied on the 13th July 1931.

The French Government claimed compensation amounting to 390,000 Indo-China piastres for the Communist damages to French property, and, in the meantime, closed its frontier to Chinese trade. This claim was somewhat reduced in subsequent negotiations, and the French Consulate and Catholic Mission buildings were repaired at Chinese expense, while the Chinese Government also reimbursed her Customs employees for their losses—the only object recovered being the Commissioner's piano, which, needless to say, was considerably out of tune!

This, then, was the position on my arrival. The trade of the port, never very prosperous, had received a serious blow, from which it was unlikely to recover for some time. However, I decided to do my best with the material at my disposal.

Shortly after my arrival, the Dragon Boat Festival was celebrated with all due ceremony in the river at the bottom of my garden. This festival is held annually on the 5th June in memory of the poet and patriot Ch'u P'ing of the fourth century B.C., who arose to champion the people against the corruption of the local officials in the realm of Tso. The Emperor failed to support him, so the disappointed leader, tired of life, drowned himself in the Mi-lo River! Boats went out in search of his body, and since then there has been an annual carnival, with races between long boats decorated like Dragons, and manned by a number of rowers who compete for banners. There is also a theory that the Dragon-boats date back even earlier to the original worship of the old Dragon as the personification of the forces of Nature. Some of these boats are worth as much as $1,500. The water through which they have passed is dipped up and applied to the face by the village maidens in the belief that it has a beautifying effect.

As I watched the boats, richly carved and coloured, with a red silk flag in the bow, and the coach in the stern beating a gong to encourage his crew, they seemed to really look like Dragons. And I thought of the Oxford and Cambridge boat race, and wondered if I would ever see it again.

I cannot say that I set the river on fire at Lungchow, the sleepiest of all Sleepy Hollows. There was little for me to do there, except to call occasionally on the Customs Superintendent, local magistrate, French Consul, and Jesuit priest, and to check over the small revenue collection. Now and again I hired a car and went to inspect the two small sub-stations.

I had a little shooting and fishing, but sport was poor. My children were at school in England, and my wife stayed there to make a home for them. After seven months of comparative idleness I began to feel rather depressed. Moreover, the climate was enervating and the food was very poor. I was beginning to suffer from intestinal pains, due, I am quite convinced, to some unpleasant Lungchow germ, and, in point of fact, necessitating a serious abdominal operation some years later. Also I had Hong Kong Foot, a fungoid disease which attacks the upper layers of the skin of the feet, and known to science by the ugly name of *Trichophytosis*!

Obviously I could not remain in good health and spirits under such adverse conditions, and, eventually, I decided to send in my resignation. I felt that my work was done, and that I ought to retire in order to give younger men a chance. I was inclined to become rather introspective, because I had little else to occupy my time. I compared myself to a lightkeeper who lived on a secluded headland of the China coast, and whose sole amusement consisted in playing an old musical-box. In spite of the fact that there was something wrong with it, and therefore tunes could only be produced *backwards*, he nevertheless obtained complete satisfaction from the inverted compositions of this remarkable instrument! I also resembled that mythical bird, likened to many of the older generation, who always flew backwards because he enjoyed what was past so much more than the prospect of what was to come!

Trade was very bad, and banks were breaking in all directions. China went off the silver standard. I found it very difficult to remit home for family expenses owing to the unfavourable rate of exchange, which was beginning its rapid fall. The Chinese dollar, which was worth two shillings when I first went out to China, finally dropped to the value of only a quarter of a farthing! I have since heard that, after the Japanese capitulation of 1945, Chinese currency depreciated to such an extent that one pound sterling equalled Chinese National $184,500 according to the official quotation in 1947, and C.N. $245,000 in the Black Market at Shanghai!

The financial depression of that time was attributed by the native soothsayers to the fact, that, according to the Chinese zodiac, the year 1935 was the year of the Pig, an animal of very bad manners, called by the fancy name of 'the long-nosed General' from its habit of poking about in everybody's gardens in the hope of picking up unconsidered trifles. Thus the pig is only useful when it is dead. Hence it was a good thing when the year of bad luck was past; but 1936 was the year of the Rat, which has an even more thieving disposition. It was clear that I had better retire before the year of the Monkey and the month of the Cat, because these animals, not being provided for at all in the Chinese cycle, correspond to the Greek Kalends. It must be now or never!

I wish I had been born in the year of the good old Dragon, but unfortunately I first saw the light in the year of the Cock, that showy and pugnacious creature, and now my cock-fighting days in China were over, and I was returning to the family farmyard to be, I hoped, the cock of my own roost. I was afraid there would be rather a shortage of corn, which had been severely rationed, but the food would be better than at Lungchow. Sometimes, after a solitary dinner of tough and unpalatable buffalo steak and stringy sweet potatoes in China, I lit my cigar and mused on the fabled region of medieval romance where the rivers are of wine, the houses of cake, and the streets of pastry, while roasted geese, fowls and buttered larks walk about asking to be eaten. Then I returned to earth and found the coffee was cold. and I was suffering from the pangs of indigestion!

Before leaving Lungchow, I went for a stroll along the river bank. It was a quiet and peaceful afternoon. Lazily, a buff-backed heron, or paddy-bird, rose from the adjoining rice-fields, and winged its way into the hazy distance. At the edge of the water the pied water wagtail, or 'dish-washer', with his black and white plumage, was bobbing up and down with his kindred, thus resembling a number of menials, in their white sleeves, washing dishes in the stream before the days of taps and sinks. And further along there were actually some peasant girls beating out their day's washing on the rocks, and drawing water for their household requirements.

With a sudden roar the daily aeroplane passed overhead *en route* for the aerodrome outside the city, and this seemed to irritate the 'One More Bottle' bird, a variety of cuckoo with a maddening voice, breaking into a monotonous chorus of *Kuei-kuei-kuo-kuo*, which rang continually in my ears until I returned home for tea.

On the eve of my departure from Lungchow, I sat on my veranda, and played a final game of chess with the French Consul. The sun sank slowly behind the bamboos in the garden. Later on the watchman began to make his rounds, marking his vigilance by sharply tapping his little wooden drum. The Dragon's children stopped playing with the 'mud-puppies' in the river, and retired to rest with their illustrious father. The night closed in, and all was still.

CHAPTER 24

L'Envoi

I awoke one morning to the realization that, for exactly thirty-two years, I had been 'sitting at the receipt of custom' in China, and that on my writing-desk lay an official dispatch from the Inspector-General of Customs recording his appreciation of the 'valuable services' which I had rendered to China and to the Customs Service for many years, and expressing the hope that my period of retirement may be a long and happy one.

Of course, as I have served at the Head Office I am well aware that this is only a stereotyped form which is addressed impartially to all retiring employees; yet, at the same time, I suppose I have, at least, earned my pay.

It may be of some interest to see how far I succeeded in following the original advice given in the open letter to a Fourth Assistant, B, in Chapter 3 of this volume.

As regards my financial position, I never got into debt, and even accumulated some savings, while I did not have to refund my passage-money.

I went home on my second leave, as foretold, with four olive-branches and a wife. Fortunately by that time the rates of pay had been increased, and the rule was that I was entitled to a year's holiday on full pay, if I preferred it to two years on half pay—which I certainly did.

Though I never served as an Inspector of Forts, and did not assume any of the other unusual duties suggested by my kind preceptor, yet I actually became—much to my own surprise—a Postal Accountant, President of the Hong Kong Foreign Women's Relief Association, Examiner in Mandarin for Hong Kong University, Vice-President of the Famine Relief Committee of Chekiang, Member of the Anti-Opium Association, Chinese Assistant Secretary, Vice-President and Lecturer at the Customs College, I.G.'s Representative on the

Examining Committee for Customs Travelling Scholarships, Laureate
of the French Academy, and Officer of the Chinese Fourth Class
Order of the Excellent Crop; which is certainly a strange collection
of miscellaneous titles.

I have been careful in my attitude towards the public. It is my
opinion that the encouragement of trade leads to the increase of the
revenue. I never accepted a bribe myself, but I often bribed a difficult
customer with a cigar. He would then eat out of my hand and pay his
duty without further demur.

I think, perhaps, I spent too much time on the Chinese language.
This, I think, induced many of my colleagues to imagine that I was
trying 'to put one over on them'! It was terribly hard work—and did
me very little good. I really think I ought to have followed the advice
of the open letter and avoided the study of Chinese as much as
possible.

Contrary to advice again, I made a close study of office procedure,
treaties, and I.G.'s Circulars, and certainly much of this material
became obsolete as time went on.

I was stationed at Peking twice, but never made love to the Minister's wife. My own wife might have objected! And I never made
friends with my Commissioner's wife with a view to her helping me
in my career—for the same reason.

Finally, referring again to the letter of advice, the only wind
instrument I ever played was my own trumpet. After all nobody else
can blow it for you!

I joined the Service as Fourth Assistant, C, in the Indoor Staff, and
gradually passed through the various other ranks of Assistant, until I
became a Chief Assistant, then a Deputy Commissioner, finally retiring with the rank of Commissioner. Very few of my contemporaries
of the old Imperial days are still alive.

Some of us were rather inclined to grumble at what we considered
as slow progress up the ladder, but, on the whole, I think we were
nearly all treated according to our deserts. Every year we were each
presented with a copy of the printed Service List, which recorded
the names and ranks of the Staff for the past year. In charge
of the Returns Office at one of my stations was a crotchety old
gentleman who was never able to rise beyond the rank of Assistant.
He invariably sent his Service List back to the Secretary by the
office-boy with this quotation from *Othello* inscribed on it in red
ink:

> ' 'Tis the curse of service,
> Preferment goes by letter and affection,
> Not by the old gradation, where each second
> Stood heir to the first!'

I can sympathize with him. Shakespeare certainly knew what he was talking about!

If I had stayed on in China for another three years, I should have qualified for a full pension and a Long Service Medal. Moreover, my passage home would have been defrayed by the Service. But I decided to waive these advantages and retire on a reduced pension.

I devoted a good deal of my spare time to the writing of various books. The most successful of these was my *Outlines of Chinese Symbolism and Art Motives*, which went into three editions. I finally sold the copyright. My *Anglo-Chinese Glossary for Customs Use* was included in all Customs Libraries, but, naturally, it is now out of date. I compiled a *Manual of Chinese Metaphor* and presented it to the Service. It was printed by order of the Inspector-General and was awarded the Prix Stanislas Julien by the French Academie, for being, in their opinion, the best book on China during the year. I drew up various textbooks on Customs Indoor and Outdoor Work, and they were published by the Customs College Press for the use of the students. At my suggestion the statistics of trade were recorded by means of coloured graphs.

In the course of my official duties, I have often been required to write reports on the trade of the various districts in which I have been stationed, and they have been printed and issued for sale to the public as Chinese Customs yellow books. I have also written for various periodicals.

My literary output was not always approved. One Commissioner stated that my *Manual of Chinese Metaphor* was 'caviare to the General'. Another accused me of being 'an admirable Crichton' when he heard that I was lecturing at the Customs College on the general duties of all ranks of the Service, from the lowest to the highest. I presented him with a printed copy of my lecture notes. When he read them perhaps he came to the conclusion that he had misjudged me. Even the Inspector-General damned me with faint praise by complimenting me on my 'capacity for turning out books', so I presume he began to find my efforts rather monotonous. I sometimes dedicated my books to the Inspector-General of the day; one of them was pleased, but another seemed quite annoyed! Apparently he was under the impression that I was trying to get some kudos by what I only intended as a respectful compliment.

A dear old lady once said to me, 'Your book on Chinese symbolism is wonderful! I haven't read it—but it's wonderful!' Of course, I advised her *not* to read it in case she might be disillusioned. Nevertheless another critic remarked, 'The only objection I have to the book is that it is *too short*!' As he was a noted sinologue, I was extremely flattered.

There are about forty Custom Houses in different parts of China, together with a number of sub-offices. I have been stationed in eleven ports, and was Acting Commissioner in four. I am very glad to have had the privilege of working for the Chinese Government. Foreign participation in Customs work is now withdrawn, and the Chinese are now in complete control of the Service. The Chinese Staff have been carefully trained and selected, and should be able to carry on the work on the lines drawn up by their predecessors, amongst whom, I am very proud to say, the British have taken the major part.

When I retired from China I dug out my passport for what may be the last time. I am glad of this because the said passport contains a photograph which has faded unevenly and now resembles a criminal with a vicious leer, and is suitable only for inclusion in the Chamber of Horrors at Madame Tussaud's. It is labelled 'Photograph of Bearer'. Although I look as if I were bearing some kind of heavy burden—perhaps an evil conscience—this classification is really inaccurate. I cannot bear it at all. It is truly terrible! And I can see that all passport officers regard it with considerable suspicion!

I have had some queer experiences when endeavouring to obtain the necessary endorsements or Consular *visa* on my passport. China and Japan were prompt and free of charge, but limited my movements to one year, although I was a Chinese Customs official myself, and China was my home for many years. America kept me waiting for hours, and filled in the details of my journey all wrong, but collected no fee. Russia, or the United Union of Soviet Republics, was very expensive, demanded six photographs (one for each Republic perhaps), and set me a lengthy written examination-paper to answer. Manchuria asked innumerable questions on both frontiers. Poland declared my photograph was libellous, to which I heartily agreed. France said it was flattering, to which I strongly objected. Indo-China was slow—and not quite certain of the necessary procedure.

I had to eat my way out of China. The local officials very kindly invited me to various farewell dinner-parties, and I was constrained to consume much variegated provender and many assorted beverages. I developed the usual symptoms of 'farewell-dyspepsia'. At my last Chinese banquet I was regaled with lotus-roots, birds'-nest soup, ancient eggs, sharks' fins, stewed fox, dog-meat, awabi (an india-rubber-like shellfish), chicken-skin pancakes, deer sinews, ducks' brains, mushrooms, water-chestnuts, sea-slugs, tadpoles, carp stuffed with onions, seaweed, fir-cones, sponge-cake in almond sauce, chrysanthemum tea, rose-leaf wine, champagne and brandy! I had to have at least two helpings of each!

I have already described the difficulties I experienced in entering the Land of the Dragon. It was quite as hard to get out of it. I booked my passage by aeroplane to Canton, with the intention of travelling thence by train to Hong Kong. The plane, however, was held up for some reason or other, chiefly blamed on military requirements.

What was I to do to avoid missing my steamer from Hong Kong? I lit my last cigar, but alas! there was no inspiration from the fragrant smoke. With my retirement from the Customs its virtue had apparently departed! I decided to give up cigars in future. They are nothing but a delusion and a snare. And, of course, I cannot afford them now.

My good friend the Tupan, the senior military official, fortunately came to the rescue, and very kindly lent me his motor car, with two soldiers to drive it, and I started off at noon on the 16th November 1935, with a howling gale blowing, and to the accompaniment of a fusillade of Chinese fire-crackers, which were set off in token of farewell by the assembled members of my office staff. They waved their hands 'to speed the parting guest'—a guest in their country for thirty-two years, or rather more than half a Cycle of Cathay.

It was a very sad moment for me, for in many parts of China I had had much happiness, and there were many friends, both Chinese and foreign, whom I was sorry to leave. I shall also miss the China shooting, especially the early-morning duck flighting I have so much enjoyed in various parts of the country. My allegiance to the Dragon was at an end.

On the whole, I suppose the world has treated me according to my deserts. 'So many people', writes Hugh Walpole in *The Inquisitor*, 'have a kind of notion that life owes them something—that it's life's duty to be kind to them and look after them. Life doesn't give a damn. No one's going to protect you or be sorry for you. You must meet your own dragons, ride your own tigers.' Well, I have made the acquaintance of the Lungchow Dragon in his native haunts, and I rode away in a smoking chariot driven by two 'Tigers'—as Chinese soldiers are sometimes called.

At three in the afternoon I arrived at Mingning and was ferried across the river in the car, arriving at Nanning at 9 p.m., after a very bumpy and chilly journey, and carrying only a small suitcase, which I had originally reserved for the aeroplane. I thanked and rewarded my two 'Tigers' and hastened to the house of Mr Manuel T. Wong, Commissioner of Customs, who very kindly gave me a hot dinner and arranged for me to go by junk to the first rapid, where he said I could board the motorboat *Yan Fung*, which would anchor there for the night.

I went aboard the *Yan Fung* at 10.30 p.m., and retired to a hard wooden bunk in a long saloon with many Chinese passengers, all snoring peacefully. I was unable to sleep, as I had no bedclothes and felt very cold. Owing to the continued and noisy vibration, these motorboats on the West River are commonly known as 'Blue-bottles'.

Only Chinese food was obtainable on board, and I hardly got enough to eat, and some of the dishes were very unpalatable. The other passengers were most friendly, and they all gathered round and watched me with great interest when I shaved every morning. The Chinese very rarely take the trouble of shaving themselves if there is no barber available.

We had two meals a day consisting chiefly of boiled fish and rice, one at 8 a.m. and the other at 3.30 p.m. In between times the passengers bought sweetmeats, fruit and *fried beetles* from small boats which came alongside at the various ports of call. I sampled a beetle, but I cannot say I really liked it. The Chinese consumed enormous quantities of them.

At 11.30 a.m. on the 19th, I arrived at Wuchow, feeling rather stiff from the wooden bunk, and exceedingly hungry, and I had an excellent lunch with the Commissioner, Mr C. B. W. Moore, and his wife, who saw me off in the Customs launch to the S.S. *Taihing* of the Kwong Wing Co., which left at 2 p.m. I slept well that night on a good spring bed after a large curry dinner, and arrived at Hong Kong on the following day at 1 p.m.

After spending a couple of days on the Peak—in my former

quarters—with Mr E. Bathurst, Deputy Commissioner, who was most hospitable, I boarded the Nord Deutscher Lloyd S.S. *Scharnhorst* and sailed for England, home and beauty, at 8 p.m. on the 22nd November, arriving at Southampton, after a splendid voyage, on the 21st December, in a thick fog and a hard white frost, after nine months of tropical weather in the East.

Just before I sailed, I received a telegram wishing me 'Bon voyage and good luck'. It was signed by the Shanghai agent of a well-known insurance company, who had just sold me a policy. I was glad to feel that there was someone deeply interested in the hazards of my life, who would be painfully grieved if I should happen to be lost in a shipwreck!

The China papers recorded my retirement with certain journalistic touches. A Shanghai publication stated that, after being a Commissioner of Customs at Tientsin for many years I had proceeded to England to undertake the education of my large family! I wish I *had* been a Commissioner 'for many years'. It took me all my time to reach that enviable position. And my family are rather inclined to educate *me*!

A Peking journal also delivered itself of the following observations: 'Another landmark in the Chinese Customs Service is the departure of Mr C. A. S. Williams, who expects to sail from Hong Kong on S.S. *Scharnhorst* on November 22nd. Mr Williams was formerly Commissioner of Customs in Peiping, prior to Mr Neprud, and recently has been stationed at Lungchow, Kwangsi. Mr Williams is leaving on retirement.' Well, I suppose the newspapers *must* live. I have been called a good many things in my time, but I have never been described as a 'LANDMARK'!

I am now in a position to compare myself to the late Mr Bardell, of the *Pickwick Papers*, who 'glided almost imperceptibly from the world, to seek elsewhere for that repose and peace which a Custom House can never afford'. But I hope I shall not be knocked on the head with a quart pot in a public house, as that retired Customs official actually was!

Though I am no longer to be classed as one of 'the world's workers' —if I ever was, I am still able to put in a good day's work in my garden. I have always looked forward to my own 'acre of land and a cow'. But I am only a 'landmark' or part of the landscape, and no longer a 'Great Man', as the Chinese used to call me when I was one of their Civil Servants. From being, as it were, a Dragon, or a

Celestial Mandarin, with almost plenipotentiary powers, I have become just an ordinary 'man in the street'. But I have had my moments, and now I have freedom from the exactitude of public service.

My travels are over. It is a blessed thing to journey, but it is even more blessed to reach the journey's end—and that means home at last!